THROW ME A ROPE, A MEMOIR
JESSICA SINGER

Printed in the United States of America

For more information,
www.booksbyjess.com

Cover design by Jessica Singer
ISBN 978-1-7336279-0-0

For my three extremely unordinary, imperfectly perfect amazing boys, and to my Captain
Thanks for putting up with my many quirky idiosyncrasies.
This means we've taught you well. Always accept others for exactly who they are.
Remember, your failures will lead to your successes—and you get to define what success means to you.

To the multitude of folks that helped me in editing, proofreading, copywriting and providing sound critiques throughout this
five-year journey, I can't possibly thank you enough—you're all treasured.

To my baby brother Tyson, thank you for being my honorary big brother. You're the real deal.

Mom and Dad, you are, and always will remain—my heroes.

CONTENTS

Jessica Singer launched Mamabargains.com right smack in the middle of the Great Recession of 2008. Securing a six-figure, yearlong partnership with a giant household-name conglomerate, Singer changed the definition of viral forever. Her grassroots strategy crashed servers, but helped to inspire a generation of budding mompreneurs. She was awarded a shiny gold Stevie Award as Women in Business' Fastest Growing Company in the nation, and Mamabargains was named to Inc. Magazine's 5000 fastest growing private companies in America in 2013. Boring, right?

Six years after her launch, the multimillion-dollar business tanked, threatening to take Singer and her family down with it. Getting to the top required every ounce of her effort and energy.

Getting *out* would take her to the very edge of insanity, despair and death's door.

Searingly honest and colorfully written—if you're sensitive to brassy language or uncensored something something's, this isn't the story for you. Singer copes with personal tragedy and public shame the only way she knows how.

The nerve. This bitch owes me $12.85 for an order I paid for but never received after she closed. Now she wants me to *buy her book?* Yes—because I wrote it for *you.*

I owe you an explanation, and within these pages, you'll find that—and more.

The following is what happens when an open book writes one.

*Many names have been changed or omitted. Fuck censorship.

1. THE LAST ARMAGEDDON SANDWICH

I've just had major surgery and arrived back home—to a place that may not be ours much longer. Our attorney warned us. He told us they could take everything. The house, the cars, all of it—was at risk.

What do we do? Will they take our kids' college savings accounts too?

Will our lives be destroyed for closing the Mamabargains doors—for trying to do the right thing?

Body parts missing from surgery, unable to walk, and high as a kite from the painkillers—I'm facing judgment day without him.

My husband, Stanford, is in The Middle East. Risking his life to make just a tiny bit extra to throw at the banks Mamabargains owes. He closes his eyes each night wondering if he'll open them again to look around the hellhole military base he'll call home for the next four months. Suicide bombers blow themselves up at its gates. People have been killed doing exactly what he's there doing.

I'd fall to pieces if Stanford never came home. We celebrated our ten-year wedding anniversary with him in The Middle East. It was festive. He couldn't get a line out and I cried myself to sleep.

Now this?

My mom is sitting on the couch drinking her coffee. She flew in just for the special occasion of multiple body parts being removed from my body.

Stanford and I don't have a shred of family here in Utah. Thank goodness for her.

Oh God. Thank goodness for my mom. There, I've said it. Of all the times I've silently cursed her and for all the times we've hated each other and gotten into fights, I still adore her. It's her imperfections that I adore the most.

Keep it together, Jess. Don't let those painkillers cloud your judgment. Keep a clear head.

Even though my mom is supposed to be wrangler-in-chief in lieu of their at the moment Oxycontin popping mom, the kids are now running around like maniacal idiots. How am I supposed to chase them around in my condition, fresh off the operating table?

Just a small shot to calm my frayed nerves. Just one. Whiskey will work.

People pay good money for this kind of drug-induced state. Actually, I'm fairly certain people have *died* from this combo. My heart is pounding outside my chest, and I'm sweating. Dehydrating with every breath. Not even the hardest of cardio workouts gets me to break a sweat, and now my ass planted on the couch awaiting the IRS grim reaper is sucking the very life out of me. Life is leaving my body in sweat droplets dribbling down my every crack and crevice.

How did we get here?

Just a few months back we won an award from Inc. magazine. We were listed as one of the top 5,000 businesses in the entire *nation*. That's a big deal. Our company won awards regularly for growth and accomplishments. We had a staff of twenty-one employees and contractors at our peak.

And then...

My mouth goes dry when I think about what they did to us. Or maybe that's a side effect of the drugs? I'm not sure on account of the whiskey. And Oxycontin. And fear laced with thoughts of revenge.

Maybe I should have another shot. Did I have a shot already?

Closing was the only responsible thing to do. It wasn't easy nor did we take it lightly. We had employees with families that lost their jobs the day we shut our doors. We had customers awaiting orders. They lost that day too, and so did some of our vendors.

"There are no winners when a business closes."

I've become cozy with the phrase lent to me by our attorney. All that's left is a bunch of losers trying to scratch their way to the surface so they can say that they learned something from the whole mess.

Those fuckers. I'll never forget what they did. It'll eat away at me until my dying day.

The IRS phoned just a few moments ago to say they were sending someone right now, and yours truly was the stupid ass to answer the phone. Mamabargains has back payroll tax debt, and from what I've heard, the IRS is gnarly, and they'll penalize you to death. It was one-quarter worth of payroll taxes—precisely the kind you never ever want to owe.

My nerves are shot, mouth is dry, entire body is wet from sweat, and I ache down below where those body parts used to be.

Resting in the small of my back is my worry rock. A small token that I keep nearby when the worry seems to overwhelm me. I carried that rock often in the year before we ultimately closed the doors to Mamabargains, six years after its inception and revenue in the seven digits at its demise. The rock is there, tucked into the waistband of my pajamas so I can feel it pressed against my back. If I can feel it there, maybe it'll take away the incessant anxiety?

Do they send people to jail for owing back tax?

"Can a person be arrested for owing taxes?" I type into the Google search bar as a trickle of liquid nervousness runs from my armpit down to my hip.

Okay, that makes me feel a bit better. Unless a crime has been committed, than no, they can't arrest you, says Google.

Wait. But what constitutes a crime?

Wouldn't *not* paying taxes constitute a crime?

Shit. Fuck.

I didn't commit a crime; we just didn't pay for one quarter.

Oh. My. God. My brain is wet dogfood—a ball of mush just waiting for this zombie IRS man to eat it alive.

This isn't going to go well.

Will the IRS man and his SWAT team search my house?

Will they take our belongings we've spent our lives collecting? I don't think I could part with the ornament of the sexy (totally unlike me) high-heeled shoes that signify the peak of business success that Stanford gave to me several years back.

And I don't even wear heels all that often. Apparently they were out of the flip-flop ornaments that day.

What if my mom says or does something she shouldn't?

My kids should look more homely.

Oh my God. I'm on drugs, what if I say something I shouldn't, instead of just thinking it? It's me I should worry about, not Mom!

I'm overcome with emotion. I can't think straight.

What's that noise?

"Shut up you damn dog! No, wait, *hide* the dog!"

He's an overly enthusiastic Goldendoodle—people who owe the IRS shouldn't be posh pooch owners.

Can dogs be repossessed?

"No, but mom, really, please hide the dog. The man will think he's a luxury item."

What about me? How expensive am I looking?

Perfect, there's a hole in the knee of my pajamas. Look dire, Jess, look dire.

Wait. I *am* dire. I don't have to pretend. I'm in a hole, our whole family is.

Just be honest, Jess. That's always been your thing, your niche. Tell it how it is. That's why the Mamabargains customers came in droves and stayed. They loved the honesty. They knew we were always straight up with them. And that's why the vendors loved working with us—we were always trustworthy. No filter.

I can't think clearly. What is that *goddamn* banging sound?

It's the door. The Tax Monster is at the door with the IRS SWAT team.

Is it too late to run with the enemy already at the gate?

Yes. Yes it is too late, because helpful Mom is already answering the door. Thanks, Mom. You're always there for me, even when I don't exactly want you to be.

I stagger to my wobbly legs and although my mouth is dry and my body soaked in sweat, I consider one final option—maybe I can try to lay the charm on and...

Oh God. I won't even be able to try and flirt my way out of this. Or, maybe...nah.

He's a she. The IRS *man* is an IRS *woman*.

She's very large and more than mean looking, and she has a *folder*.

Oh My God. It's thick as shit too. Stuffed with our non-existent tax crimes. Oh my God. Nooooo!

Why couldn't they have sent a man? I think a man I could muster some tears for and he would take pity upon my poor, poor soul. A woman, well, women can be cutthroat bitches. I know, because I've been one—a cutthroat bitch. But to be a woman in her position at the IRS, she's likely five times the nightmare that any man could dream of being. I'm certain she'll be five times as cruel, heartless, and unforgiving. I'm screwed.

IRS woman has long, brown hair. Stick straight, and to be honest, it looks greasy. Like *really* greasy. No way did she shower today. Her pantsuit is a bit crumpled at the legs, and the pants are way too short. Her shoes are brown and tattered. Probably shit remnants from all of her ass kicking. What I have in front of me is nothing short of a terrifying joke. She doesn't appear to be much older than me, maybe in her mid-40s? To have frown lines living that deeply on her otherwise flawless skin made me wonder...

What makes her frown so much?

That's easy—people like me who owe the government money.

No spoken words for a few moments, just the sounds of thoughts racing through my drugged up brain. The nail on chalkboard sound of her rustling through all of the papers in that dastardly folder on her lap was no picnic, either. It seems like ten minutes of nothingness. In reality, it's probably a minute, maybe two. But at least there've been no catastrophes yet. Scratch that.

My three-year-old comes barreling into the room, crazy toddler flips onto the couch, and crash lands directly onto IRS woman's lap. The entire contents of her folder of death scatter about the room. I'm speechless. Literally nothing that sounds good in my head will come out correctly. I have no idea how to parent this toddler at the moment, especially with an audience like her. I just stare at him, hoping she doesn't see my big evil eyeballs looking him square in his cute little green peepers.

Despite the Oxycodone, the whiskey, and the sweat, my silent stare of death does the trick, and off he slinks, or did I just imagine all of that?

IRS woman makes an aggravated 'uhhuh' sound as she gathers the papers, followed by an indecipherable 'Hmmnghah.'

What does that *mean*?

It's burning! She's burning me with her laser eyes!

Her stare of death is far more diabolical than mine. Clearly, I'm an amateur.

Stop it! Stop staring at me with those judgey mean IRS lady red eyes!

I wish I could slink away with my possibly imagined three-year-old into the clever bribery room that's been set-up by mom to keep the kids occupied. It's overflowing with cookies, candy, movies and too many other privileges to mention—but now isn't the time to worry about diabetes and obesity. The bribes aren't working. The other two boys (nine and seven) are standing in front of me demanding the password to the family timer on their video game console.

Before you can say "luxury electronic item to be seized by the IRS" the extravagant eighty-pound dog comes prancing through the room with his toy. His favorite toy—the super slobbery one. Posh Pooch chooses this moment to demonstrate his athleticism and fervor for trashing my carpet. He launches off of, and then knocks over, my nice sitting chair as he throws his body over the top of the coffee table. Luxury item noted. Panting and drooling, he drops the slobber-covered ball at the IRS lady's tattered brown ass-kicking shoes.

Come on lady, look at that adorable fluffy face. He doesn't deserve to be out on the street with his mom in prison, right?

I don't know the difference in these moments, between reality, and imagined fear. What's real and what isn't? Only the oxy will know.

IRS lady is clearly a cat person. She looks unamused and unimpressed with my dog's sheep-like leaping ability and couldn't care less about his future.

When does that SWAT team arrive to end this agony? I'm not only the proud recipient of her laser eyes, but a downturned mouth that looked ready to scream obscenities my way any moment. So that's why she frowns. The Jessica's of the world do it to her.

In my imagination, I picture Mom deciding to speak, "Can I make you a sandwich? Would you like anything to drink?" she asks Laser-Eyes. A fucking *sandwich*, Mom?

Shhhh! Keep it together, Jess. You can do this. You've accomplished great things in your life; this is just a little hurdle.

First thing: These drugged-up conversations within yourself need to stop, and you need to concentrate on the job at hand before mom offers the IRS lady a room for the night and a foot massage.

In reality, IRS lady speaks, "Mrs. Singer? You owe the IRS a large sum in back payroll taxes. You realize that this is a crime, correct?"

"I, well, ye..." Hastily stopping mid sentence to blow my nose and wipe the tears pouring down my cheeks.

Come on, Jess! You can do this! Don't cry. Be tough as nails.

"I realize we owe one quarter in payroll taxes, Ma'am. We never paid late, and when the business was at a point of no return, we limited ourselves. We set a ceiling for ourselves at which point we would no longer drain ourselves financially, and we hit that ceiling. Two weeks later, we stopped. We sold a car to pay for one payroll period. We drained the only savings account we had left to pay a few vendors with, and then there was the IRS. It's a lot of money to us, and we feel horrible that we owe it."

IRS lady's expression said she'd heard it all before, "Mrs. Singer, I'm here on behalf of the Internal Revenue Service and all of the other tax paying citizens in our great country to uphold the law regarding your decision to *not* pay your taxes. It's people like you that ruin it for everyone else. Now, let's get to it, tell me exactly how this happened".

Okay lady, you asked for it. Maybe you should buckle up and have that sandwich.

"Do you want the summary, or the unabridged version?"

How did we get here?

How'd we go from nothing to successful and than back again?

Well, as corny as it sounds, this multi-million dollar journey all started with a dream. On March 20th, 2008, I had an honest to goodness, crazy-ass dream.

Oh gawd. I think I just saw you roll your eyes. Yes, that was an eye roll, wasn't it? Couldn't be mistaken for anything else. Just let me continue. I promise, it gets good.

I couldn't shake it. I just couldn't let the dream go, and so several weeks later, I decided to share it with my husband.

I have to share the whole story. It's my story. These self-dialogues within me are enough to confuse anyone, but the devil/angel arguing on each shoulder seem to be doing a pretty good job at keeping me on task—for now at least.

The dream wasn't my first stab at entrepreneurship. That obsession started at a much younger age. The oldest of three, with two younger brothers, I was a leader.

My parents both worked their asses off for the little that we had. While the other girls were curling their hair, putting makeup on and doting over boys, I was busy getting sap in my hair, climbing trees, building things with my hands, playing baseball, doing gymnastics and riding my BMX bike. Tomboy, much?

See, I grew up in a trailer park. We lived in a 'double-wide.' Those singlewides were for the white trash down the road. Our doublewide—that was luxurious. To be quite honest, I loved that damn house. We lived in a clean, well-kept neighborhood, right smack in the middle of redneck town, in hodunk Graham, Washington, until I was in Fifth Grade.

Graham may have been dull, but it seemed to attract an abundance of colorful residents.

One neighbor was a child molester—we called him M&M. Like the rapper, but not. And nothing at all like the candy. I have no idea why that was his nickname, but his crater-laden face, and tall creeper stature has stuck with me my entire life. He did things.

Another neighbor was a little mentally unstable. Linda was about eight years old. She lived in the double wide at the very end of our street. One time sweet little Linda told us she had something to show us. "Hey, come check out the new trick I taught my dog!" She walked us to her laundry room, lay on the floor, and invited her poor little skin and bones Chihuahua over to lick her nether regions. Poor dog. Was probably his only meal that day. Shudders. I'm permanently scarred.

When Def Leppard's song, 'Pour Some Sugar On Me' came on the radio, she did as instructed. I can't hear that song today without thinking of Linda covering herself in sugar. Her older sister, Kelly, would sit on the couch and stare into space, bouncing forcefully against the back of the couch or chair. Years after we moved, Linda and Kelly's mother committed suicide, couch-bouncing sister Kelly died, and I wondered if the neighborhood surroundings had anything to do with it. You can't make shit like that up. For living in a decent, completely functional, but dysfunctional neighborhood, we sure had fucked up neighbors.

Jesus, when I put it into words, how the hell did I survive? Somehow I turned out mostly fine. Ahem.

From homely little size zero beanpole Jess, to successful business owner. I think I realized at about six that I didn't want to get eaten alive by all that the Graham, Washington life was threatening me with, so I decided I'd be the one to take control of my destiny.

While the neighborhood became stranger, I craved normalcy. Where were the kids that played jacks? Where were the ones that just wanted to climb trees? Instead, my neighbors set the trees on fire and touched each other in the creepy woods behind our houses.

I loved gymnastics, and I wanted to share what I was being taught at the local rec. center with all my neighborhood friends, so I started a gymnastics camp for the kids in the summers. Well, for the ones who weren't pyros or dog-lovers...

And no, this wasn't for the sake of being a neighborly, Good Samaritan. I had profits in mind—big profits.

I charged $2 per kid for a whole summer of lessons. I had all of my bases covered, and the parents in the neighborhood loved me. Probably because I took care of their kids in our backyard once a week, giving them time to do whatever the hell it was they did when their kids were out of the house for an hour or so.

It was all profit, no overhead. My dad built a balance beam out of old railroad ties—and then he covered it in carpet to protect my client's tiny fragile feet. I'll never forget him doing that for me. Especially since then I was able to invest some of my profits into Lionel Ritchie. That's right, I bought my very own "Dancing on the Ceiling" tape to go along with that awesome cassette tape player mom and dad bought me for Christmas.

Of course, I'm kicking myself now, because being a parent, I know what happens when the kids are gone for a bit in the middle of a weekend day. What a valuable service I was providing! Parent sex is hard to come by! My only regret is that I didn't charge more—much, much more, for my entrepreneurial gymnastics day camp. I know those parents would've paid up so they could hump like animals or snort their lines while their kids were busy learning to be vanilla next door.

Still living it up in our fancy schmancy doublewide after teaching gymnastics class in the summers, the Washington rain would set in. I needed something else. This whole trailer-park-living thing was really getting to me; I needed something to keep me busy—to make me feel in control of my own destiny. Plus, Lionel had a new album out and he needed the royalties from my lowly little tape purchase, didn't he? Making huckleberry jam by smashing it inside a plastic bag and then adding a spoonful of sugar seemed promising. But mom hated me stealing her sugar, probably thought I was going to pour it on myself or something, not to mention the labor involved in picking those damn little things was quite taxing.

In Washington State, clay was abundant. Eureka!

The answer for my next business was underfoot the entire time.

No overhead, just my time. I'd dig for hours in the rain soaked ground. I did so in every yard in our neighborhood—the rain made it easier to dig. With the materials I mined with my hands, I made little teapots and cups. Market research with the neighbors, why not?

What would they buy?

What kind of clay trinkets would they be interested in purchasing from me?

It was a pretty damn brazen endeavor for a little kid to go door-to-door selling handmade pots that were literally of *no use*. I sold them to all of the neighbors and at garage sales.

Those pots probably went straight into the trash, but I really didn't care. I felt like I'd made myself a little piece of pie. I was doing my own thing. I wasn't attached to a screen—we only had one TV and it was reserved for shows we weren't allowed to watch. I wasn't entitled. I fucking earned it.

The lemonade stand type of concept worked for me. Making things with my hands, or using my own innate skills seemed to be the best, most lucrative option. Plus, George Michael's new album, 'Faith' was out, and I'd been saving up for it.

It was near my eleventh birthday when I finally saved enough money to buy George and spring for the tape by that really cool boy band, New Kids on the Block. Thank you George, Jordan, Jonathan, Danny, Donnie, and Joey (oh Joey!) for the inspiration. If it wasn't for me wanting you so desperately, things might've not gone the way they did. And your poster above my bed serenaded me every night before sleep, Joey, so thanks for that.

Next, I started a babysitters club. The books by the same name were popular at that age for my friends and I, and it was a brilliant concept. I was a leader. Organizing it was a pain in the ass, but the neighborhood girls loved me. Not sure my parents loved all the phone calls coming to our house as I prioritized and scheduled the babysitting club girls' schedules, but it was a necessary part of growing this new endeavor.

It was no longer just me; I'd become a Human Resources Manager and a Client Advocate, at the ripe age of eleven. That pain in the ass family down the road that would 'forget' to pay the babysitter, or the ones who would cancel at the last minute? I didn't know what to do with those people, but knew they were more trouble than this job was worth. Okay, so this went well, but not nearly as well as it appeared to work in the books.

The overhead for Jess' Babysitters Club was simply the local phone calls from parents and the calls I made to the girls to schedule them. I had four girls that were on my list and we had ten families that we regularly rotated babysitting for. We charged a whole $2 per hour at the time. In hindsight, I should've taken more of a profit for myself, but I was eleven and not the fully formed business shark I now am. I could've made a boatload had I just taken 15% instead of 5% off the top of what the girls were paid each time they babysat. I was doing 90% of the work and not paying myself for my hard work. Some pimp I was!

Many years, almost straight A's throughout school and several 'real' jobs later, in 2005, I started a graphic design business called 'Life Kisses You', where I created personalized artwork. The husband and I were living in Las Vegas and I was married, with a newborn in tow. My first creation was the birth announcement for our son. I was the only designer, handling all aspects of the small venture. I absolutely loved this job, creating for others. Low overhead, little to no stress, and designing was one of my passions.

I taught myself how to use Photoshop by watching online tutorials. My overhead cost on the business was the cost of paper, my time and the software. I figured out with each new idea and venture how easy it is to have your own gig. I discovered how to track costs, which enabled me to run the show while always thinking things completely through. The big picture stayed in front of me always.

I'm a bit of a spreadsheet whore. Every cost gets tracked to the penny so as to accurately calculate out of pocket vs. total revenue vs. profit percentages. I don't make a decision without first determining the financial impact it will have.

In January 2006, we moved our small little family to Utah from Nevada. The thought of our little guy asking what XXX spells bothered me, plus...the mountains. Beautiful! We wanted to raise our family in an area where the weekend past time wasn't gambling, sweating in the stench of the summer heat, and staring at the stark, vast desert environment.

In January 2008, I became a stay at home and had a second baby, another boy.

My next venture came from my dream (the one you were rolling your eyes over). The dream became much more than a venture, it was a lifestyle. It was a blessing, and a curse. It was like a third arm, an extension of my own body and being. This next business inhabited my body similar to the way your kidneys do. Vital when healthy, but when it becomes sick, or diseased, you need to rid your body of it's existence. Make it quick, though, or you'll die in the process.

The dream became known as Mamabargains.com.

Each time I write the word, I get butterflies and nausea all at once. It makes me cry/laugh while screaming the words 'fuck you universe' into the nearest pillow laden with slobber from every other time I screamed into the goddamned thing.

I dreamt it. How ridiculous does that sound? If you dream it, it will happen, right? MLK had a dream, why couldn't I? Well, not always, but this rare time, it did happen. Didn't Jeff Bezos dream the concept of Amazon? Okay, maybe not, but I'm certain that there are other entrepreneurs out there that began with a simple dream, the sleeping, literal kind, and made themselves a success as a result.

Mrs. Mamabargains dreamt of Mamabargains, and then went and made it reality.

By March 2008 I couldn't seem to shake that weird, recurring dream.

I needed to share it with my logical, left-brained engineer husband who overthinks everything and then rethinks it even after he's made a decision. I needed to wait for the right moment to bring it up to Stanford. My gut was telling me the dream was a gift to our family.

In it, I was sitting at a computer, looking up at Stanford. I say to him, "We've had 10,000 hits already today, babe!" When I look back at the computer screen, I see a website called 'Momazon'.

That was it. That was what I'd been dreaming since late February 2008. It continued to haunt me almost nightly and only stopped when I finally shared it with Stanford. I took that as a sign as well. I'd been sitting on the dream pondering, realizing that unless we wanted legal heat from Amazon, we couldn't actually use the Momazon name.

I shared the dream with my equal half when we were on our way to a party on March 20th, 2008. He looked at me without rolling his eyes once, kind of funny at first, almost like a cartoon character. And then I saw the light bulb pop up over his head. "Why not do something like Steepandcheap.com but for *moms*?" he said.

And that was it. I'd picked my moment, and Stanford came through for me. It was my dream, combined with his ideas and encouragement that created what was soon to be known as Mamabargains.com.

Hold up. What's SteepandCheap.com?

Steep and Cheap is an ODAT (one deal at a time) website that caters to gear heads—people who love the outdoors—that want great deals on outdoorsy equipment and clothes. On their site, products like snowboards, ski jackets and even socks are all priced sometimes up to 80% off retail. Sound familiar? If you knew Mamabargains.com, it definitely does—and nowadays, there are a myriad of other 'deal sites' out there. Their concept stemmed from our idea, which stemmed from the Steep and Cheap concept.

The Singer family was addicted to Steep and Cheap. We were hooked, obsessed.

My two-year-old knew the UPS driver by name.

When that big brown UPS truck came rolling up our street in suburban Salt Lake City, he would shout, "Schuyler is here! Schuyler is here!" It was almost daily that we were receiving some sort of package—usually from Steep and Cheap, but always from some online site I shopped.

Don't judge. I was a stay at home mom with a two-year-old and a newborn. I needed something to keep me feeling alive and engaged with the outside world, especially when it was 80% off retail. Being home washing diapers, keeping a clean house and sewing doilies is just not enough for my overactive brain, and it's okay to need more. Plus I didn't even know how to sew.

I bought everything useful online from diapers to a couch. Let's not discuss the bug vacuum. What? I hate spiders, okay?

Since I detested the malls, I'd purchase from the comfort of my home sitting on that couch I bought online. I never paid full price, either. I only bought items on sale. You know, 'practically free' as Stanford liked to say. I think he was kind of pissed that he came home to new packages everyday, but he was just as guilty as I was. His purchases were less practical than mine, like that third snowboard. We needed a bug vacuum way more than another snowboard. But, alas, it was on sale!

At the party that night, we did some market research on my dream. In between the delicious food and the drinking, we asked our friends what they thought. The idea was received well, "Hell yeah, that's a great idea!" was the general consensus.

But well-wishing, slightly drunk friends is one thing, what happened next to catapult us into action?

By Friday, March 21st, 2008, I was overwhelmed with ideas, plans, brainstorming and chatting away with everyone closest to me. Here's where we met resistance. More than one family member told us we were crazy and that the idea basically sucked. That it sounded like a far-fetched business disaster waiting to happen. It didn't deflate me. Nothing could deflate this baby.

This dream is going to be a fucking reality. I make things happen.

I just knew by this stage I'd make this happen too.

Even though it was stressful, and ended in shambles, this is a story I love to share, the Mamabargains story.

By Saturday, March 22nd, 2008, I was ready to start looking at domain names. I began my nearly six straight hours search on GoDaddy looking for the perfect name for our dream business. The name was vital. Find one that is catchy and stands out. The name should clearly explain the business and its purpose.

Mommysale.com – taken

Mommyshit.com – too...stinky.

Momgoods.com – not available

Parentsteals.com—Nope. Not stealing parents.

Babysdeals.com – promising – but, we weren't selling babies, and babies weren't the shoppers we were targeting.

I felt like we were trying to come up with a name for our first-born child. It was a lot harder than I thought it'd be!

Until I found:

Mamabargain.com – awesome, but it's not just one bargain only we wanted to offer.

Mamabargains.com? Mamabargains.com!

Holy shit. I couldn't believe the name was available!

I was confused that such a great name wasn't already being used. Was there something wrong with it I couldn't see? It's like a house you get a great deal on, but then sit and wait for the roof to cave in. It felt too good to be true. I also couldn't believe that such a perfect domain name was less than ten bucks!

So at four in the morning, I bought mamabargains.com. Our future banked on one single domain name.

It's happening.

Remember this later, because this was my *very first mistake* as a new business owner. I'll share with you what to do and what to avoid business-wise in a later chapter.

I woke Stanford up after the purchase of our baby, Mamabargains, took her first breath. Afterwards, we fucked like rabbits. When I told him I'd found the perfect name, apparently that turned him on. It was a memorable too, the first time since I'd birthed our second baby back in January 2008. Having a newborn and toddler, and healing from a gaping hatchet vagina wound from delivery kept me uninterested in sex for exactly seventy-two days, but who's counting? Except maybe poor, horny Stanford. This is a day I'll never forget. We didn't make love, we downright...

...You get the picture.

When I woke on Monday morning my search for vendors began. I still hadn't solidified what we were going to do, in what order, and what would happen or not happen as a result. I was 100% winging it at that point. As an entrepreneur, you've got to do just that and trust that the risks you're taking will eventually pay off. Or fail. It's a 50/50 chance. Do you like roulette?

I scoured the net for our first product. If we were modeling the business on Steep and Cheap, we needed to find merchandise that could be sold to us at a discount off of wholesale.

I found an interest in the very first company I called—a brand of high-end diaper bags. I called the company and asked for a sales manager. I was thinking while I was on hold, *I'm a total fucking idiot with no damn clue what I'm doing...*

So I hung up.

I was seriously about to shit my pants. I didn't know why, but the butterflies and anxiety inside my stomach had me nearly vomiting. I knew the concept inside-out already. Mamabargains was just like Steep and Cheap, but for mom, kid and baby. Easy, right? But when it came down to it, I was terrified of the execution of the concept. It wasn't clay pots and babysitting. This was real, and it was going to make or break our family. I'd hit my first speed bump with the phone call.

My phone rang a few moments later and I thought, *Wow, that's dedication*, because the sales manager for the diaper bag company was calling me back. Fucking caller ID. I answered in my most professional voice, "Thank you for calling Mamabargains.com, this is Jessica."

This call was profound. It was as easy as a loose poop after three cups of coffee kind of easy. I'd been terrified for nothing. I explained my concept, telling him that I was looking for a discount off of wholesale pricing, that my goal was to sell the bags at 50-80% off retail.

He didn't even hesitate.

He told me that he had five hundred-diaper bags sitting in his warehouse that were being discontinued. They'd been looking for just this type of resource to move them all, but hadn't found a viable option—until I called.

"What price-point would you like to buy them for to meet your margins?"

Caught me off guard with that one.

Margins? Oh fuck. I knew he'd throw me a curveball!

I hadn't thought that far in advance, so I point-blank tossed a number out there, "We'll need at least 75% off retail." That's exactly half of wholesale as long as wholesale is 50% off retail.

To offer such a deep discount to our customers, those numbers would have to work. I hope he couldn't see that I was plucking them out of my ass. If we were going to see a profit margin for our company in the rough neighborhood of 10-25%, 75% or more would have to become our standard structure. Math whiz or not, it seemed like a good starting point.

"Sure, that sounds great. I think I can make those numbers work. Let me speak to management and I'll call you back," He said.

I waited, and then some. The day passed and he didn't call back... *Probably too steep of a discount I was asking. Damn it!*

I sent the salesman a follow-up email the next morning, just to put my name at the top of his email inbox. I was a little bummed at that point, but explained to Stanford that the company has five hundred diaper bags that each retail for $150. Stanford's response wasn't the encouragement I'd hoped for.

"Holy shit, Jess! Do you know how *much* that is?"

Fair enough, he was worried about the state of our one and only savings account with the grand total of $3,600 in it.

Realizing there was no way we could afford that, I moved on with my search. I didn't make many more phone calls. I just anxiously waited. When the phone rang three days later, I wasn't sure whether to be nervous or excited.

I opted for the latter. Stanford and I decided together that we'd follow each other into what could turn out to be complete darkness. We were unsure. What we did know was that we had only $3600 in our savings account. That's it, that's all we had to work with, and we were both willing to risk it all on Mamabargains.

What happened next catapulted us. It pushed us to certain success.

The diaper bag salesman asked if we could pay for them within the month and get them out of his warehouse. They'd work with us on pricing, realizing that to take all five hundred as a brand new business would be very risky for us. I told them one thing, and one thing only: My budget is $3600.

"If you can make that number work, get back to me." I sounded like a cutthroat businesswoman, right then and there.

A few days later, we decided that Mamabargains needed a mentor. Someone who'd been there, done that, and knew what they were doing. Someone whose brain we could pick.

What about the owner of Steep and Cheap? He's also the owner of multiple deal sites and Backcountry.com. We had to meet this guy, I didn't care how or when, but we needed to meet him. We needed to go directly to the source.

I searched online for hours. I had no idea if I'd actually find what I was looking for, but it was worth a shot. I was looking for his email address, or phone number, something—anything that would lead me directly to him.

In my search, I learned about who he was. His name was John Bresee. Many multi-millionaires aren't, but John seemed like a man of integrity, someone who loved the outdoors, who saw a need, jumped on it, and created a booming business. The money poured in through the ceiling for him. The success was vast and fast, and continued to grow. John seemed to remain humble throughout. He stayed true to his core. He stayed John.

Bingo! At last I found an email address for him. It was like I'd won the damn lottery. I remember the butterflies I felt in my stomach when I found an article that had it listed. The article was old, so who knew if the email address would even work? We needed professional guidance, and most of all I needed someone objective that I could run this whole crazy-ass idea past. Having John here in Utah was the best gift ever. Another pipedream, but a simple one worth chasing.

Just email the guy, Jess. Maybe you'll get lucky and he'll respond. Just be simple, concise, and hit the SEND button!

To: John Bresee

From: Jessica Singer

Subject: A badass idea for a badass company

John,

I have a badass idea that utilizes the Steep and Cheap concept but for a different market. Aren't you at least a little bit curious?

Ciao,

Jessica Singer

I prepared myself for the wait.

Tick. Tock.

Holy poop from a man named Jesus, John responded, and on a Saturday night, no less, mere hours from when I reached out!

Jessica,
Of course I'm curious, curiosity is my nature. Let's meet. Contact my office and they'll schedule a time for us to meet.
- John

I needed to think this opportunity through.

We had the idea, but no idea what we were doing.

But we were smart. We'd scored a major contact with someone who was both an inspiration, and a pro. We needed this.

John was the nudge the universe introduced to us.

Calling his office the following Monday, his secretary said, "John wanted me to ask that you come with your business plan in hand." We scheduled the meeting and the call was over as fast as it had begun.

Shit. A business plan?

I began working on a business plan, even though I 'd never written one before. There's a first time for everything, though, right? This was the time for me to lose my business plan virginity.

I worked for a few days, non-stop on it, Googling and YouTubing every tutorial I could find. I was teaching myself something new, and it was inspiring me to make something of this opportunity.

Like teaching myself Photoshop, I knew it was a skill that I needed that school hadn't prepared me for. You don't write business plans in high school. I wish we had. It certainly would've helped with structuring a solid plan. Considering investment opportunities down the road, being aware of competition and their strengths and weaknesses, scalability of the business, but...

Apparently that was what college was for.

I wouldn't know.

The meeting upon us, sparkly new business plan in hand, dressed to kill, Stanford and I drove to John's office.

We were petrified! I felt the incessant need to pee my pants the entire time we waited in the lobby to meet this hugely successful professional who we deeply admired. Not to mention the fact that we were only familiar with his company because we were its number one customers.

Package deliveries multiple times a week, we wanted to turn it around, making money instead of spending it.

Steep and Cheap afforded the Singers gear we wouldn't have been able to afford with the steep discount. We wanted families to have the same benefit on gear they might've not been able to afford otherwise, better yet, try brands they likely hadn't heard of before.

This is going to happen, this going to happen. We will make this happen, I'll make this happen. That chant I carried with me many other days throughout the following years.

Even now, I'm chanting....

I was honestly surprised at how low-key John was. Not all successful men look and act like Donald Trump. John wore khaki pants, New Balance sneakers and a t-shirt with a fleece zip up over it. It was so casual. I was immediately at ease, but overdressed in my stuffy white ruffle blouse. Thankful I hadn't forgotten my deodorant, and that the top button wasn't stiffly fastened, we introduced ourselves.

So far so good.

I handed John the business plan first. The one I worked tirelessly on for days before I was ready to call it complete. He glanced at it for an entire thirty seconds.

I was crushed. I'd spent hundreds of hours perfecting the damn thing.

He flipped through several pages of it, not appearing to take the time to fully read its contents.

Well fuck, he hates the idea.

The sweat swelled up in my pits, a knot formed in the back of my throat. I felt like I was interviewing for a job I knew I wasn't qualified for.

John tossed my detailed business plan on his desk, kicked his feet up beside it, and looked at us for a few seconds. The only words he'd spoken were during the informal introductions in the first moments he walked into his office, and now he took me completely by surprise.

"I love it."

"I'm sorry?"

"It's a great concept, I can't wait to see what you do with it. Why don't you meet back up with me in, say, June, and we'll see what you've been able to accomplish?"

Did he read my executive summary? What about the market analysis, or financial projections? Probably not. But who cares.

Not what I was expecting, but I took it for face value. We agreed to stay in touch, with every intention to—except things didn't quite work out that way after a brush with suspected espionage that I'll go into later.

John was generous enough to offer concrete guidance in addition to his previous compliment.

He spoke to us about the concept, about making it reality. He explained to us how he tracked costs and profits. We eventually used that simple advice to build our own customized spreadsheet that would give us the same information, plus some, in a simplified format. That document we created from John's guidance is a gold mine. It took us four full years to get it to its completed state, constantly making changes and adjustments so that it provided exactly what we needed. Data is the lifeblood of businesses like ours.

John *was* our last nudge. He was just what we needed *when* we needed it. The vote of confidence we craved.

It's all pretty surreal thinking back on those moments, the feelings and challenging decisions we had to make back then. This was an unheard of concept in the mom demographic. There were no ODAT's (One Deal at a Time) in the mom space. None. Not yet.

I called the diaper bag company back the day after our meeting with John and told them quite simply, again, that all we had to work with was $3600—that we'd love to work with them, but that was all we had. I had to reiterate the fact that there were no other funds we could gather for the purchase as a small startup. I was reaching—sticking to my guns.

I was floored when they actually agreed to sell us *all five hundred-diaper* bags for that amount.

You do the math.

Without that deal, Mamabargains.com wouldn't have been born.

I have them to thank for giving us that push, just as much as John at Backcountry.

I'm so grateful to that company for giving us that very first chance.

Years later, I found out that the sales manager who approved the deal to us was fired for doing so. Apparently he wasn't supposed to sell diaper bags to us for $7.20 a piece. He knew that they were looking to get rid of them and he was a newer employee, so he took the first deal that came across his desk. Our deal. Yay us! Sorry, nice Salesman. I hope you've gone onto bigger and better things. I'll always remember you.

The look on Schuyler, the UPS driver's face when he arrived with box after box after box in one huge diaper bag shipment was priceless. He said, "What the hell on God's green Earth did you buy *now*, woman?"

It was a funny moment that began the adventure of a lifetime. "Oh, just a few diaper bags, Schuyler," and I opened a box to show him the contents. He just looked at me, puzzled, and I could read his thoughts, 'this woman's poor husband. What the hell is she going to do with all these diaper bags? They can't even park their car in the garage, now. I'd love to be a fly on the wall when he gets home from work!'

The boxes just kept coming, filling my garage, stuffed to the gills, from floor to ceiling, wall to wall. Oh my God. There was no going back now.

I'm a procrastinator, but work fucking well under pressure.

Hundreds of diaper bags, and we *didn't even have a website* created yet.

The race was on, with too much to do and an anxiety creeping up I hadn't ever experienced before. I felt like we had little time to complete it— like something/someone was chasing us. If we didn't make this happen, someone else certainly would.

How do you build a website when you haven't a lick of coding ability?

Next, began our search for someone to build the Mamabargains website so we could start selling our merchandise.

My brother had a developer buddy, so we called on him, excited, he agreed to take on our project. Several weeks in, and no progress made on the development, we realized the guy was in way over his head, drowning under a website wish list he had no clue how to build. This could mean certain disaster for us.

Was it all over before it even began?

I'm not hocking diaper bags on the street corner, that much I was certain of.

All I could think about was the product burning a 'hole' in my 'pocket'. My pocket, though, was the entire garage stacked to the ceiling with diaper bags. I suppose plan B could be to sell them on eBay. I wonder how long it would take to sell five hundred diaper bags? Nope, There was no plan B. Not an option.

Next came my desperate plea on Elance, a website where you can post developer work that you need done. We'd wasted several weeks already with the one in over his head—time was ticking.

Our Elance search came back quick, within less than a day, with a developer in Texas who contacted us and told us he could take on the project. To our relief, he was able to get the site development underway the next day. He listened to our every need to get Mamabargains up and running quickly.

Only a solid week and a half of development, and Mamabargains.com was ready for launch.

Whenever I tell this story I relive that epic day so many years ago.

My heart is pumping. I've entered a time machine, walking in my own shoes on that very day. I thought that life was an adventure before the birth of Mamabargains. I realized that life adventures seem to come in tidal waves. I was going to surf the shit out of this one. Surf, or drown...

At 1am on May 19th, 2008, Mamabargains.com went live.

Our dream had become reality.

It may not have been Momazon, but it was a living, breathing 'thing'. Soon, it took on a life of its own. I wondered what it would become? How many years it would exist? Would our kids own it someday? What about *their* kids?

I was determined to build a legacy.

My brother was Mamabargains' first customer. It felt great that our inaugural purchaser was blood, even if he only bought one of the five hundred diaper bags, which he didn't even need. The party was on—only four hundred ninety nine to go.

Reluctant nostalgia is what I feel as my keystrokes materialize into these words.

Marketing. I had to market this beast. How was I going to make sure that the vendors whose products I'd procured would be satisfied with my sales pitch *and* come back for more? I had to build relationships. I had to get the word out.

I logged into my accounts on the mom websites and forums I belonged to, and *shamelessly promoted* Mamabargains.com.

I posted about Mamabargains from a customer standpoint. We were a lean and mean start-up, and I think this must be standard practice to a newbie business owner with zero dollars in the marketing budget. If it's not standard practice, it damn well should be. Every new customer gained is vital in the early stages. You're creating customer lifetime value. Grow the value. Win them. They'll market *for you.*

'I just found this awesome website'

'Has anyone heard of this website, Mamabargains.com?'

'I just bought a $150 diaper bag on Mamabargains.com for $29!'

It *worked*. It *really* fucking *worked.*

Orders came in almost immediately. We averaged one to two orders per day in the first few weeks. The following months our orders increased to roughly ten per day. I was ecstatic.

At the three-month mark, we'd reached five hundred *plus* orders a month. The achievement was astonishing.

It was all happening so fast. My husband, Stanford would work all day and then come home from work to help me package in our garage at night after we put our toddler and infant to bed for the night.

A beautiful beginning to our success.

The support was overwhelming. I'll forever be especially grateful for those first several companies (owners) that took a chance on Mamabargains, supporting us for what later would be known as our six years in business. The semi-truck full of product from Eurobaby, the unique items from Me In Mind Footwear, the mom owned boutique, Taylor Joelle. Dogwood Clothing, a line of apparel just for boys. Rockin' Baby slings, Uppababy strollers. After those first few vendors, hundreds more came knocking.

And people were talking. Even People Magazine - Celebrity Babies wrote about Mamabargains, only a week after our launch.

Word was spreading. Mamabargains helps you move discontinued items. Mamabargains sells your overstock within mere minutes. Mamabargains is *hot*. Soon, my outgoing cold-calls lessened in frequency— I had a hard time keeping up with all the vendors that were coming directly to us. They needed us, just as much as we needed them.

A sad aching is what I feel now. A yearning for yesterday.

I truly miss what we built. I miss it all so much that it physically pains me, bringing tears to my eyes at times when I think back.

In our first year, we grew several hundred percent. We were written about in multiple places online, won awards, and gained a credibility that followed us for six years.

How?

I'd answer customer service calls and emails at any time of the day those first two years. 2am? Sure. 11pm, why not? Mom is nursing and awake, and she has a question about the diaper bag being featured right now. I'm a mom. I've been up shopping at 2am. Sometimes that's the only productive time a new mom has. Baby is sleeping, the world is sleeping around her, and mama can finally concentrate on some bargains. A vendor would call, weary from months of trying to move out of season merchandise. I'd answer.

I wanted these shoppers, these moms, to understand that I under*stood* them, because I *was* them.

Around the clock, no customer or vendor was left without an answer to his or her inquiry. This is how I was going to grow this business and keep people talking about it. I was attached at the hip to my phone. I spent about sixteen hours or more a day working and sleeping for very short periods of time. I was on a high. Unable to stop, the addiction to business ownership took hold. I was a fucking nutcase. Mamabargains was my baby—my third little baby, and she needed me.

I had two babies already, and a husband. You know, real, living, breathing, and loving people.

Mamabargains was a drug, injected straight into my veins, seething through my bloodstream.

I was the 'mama' of Mamabargains.

She (the business) didn't love me. She filled some sort of a void I had, but like a relationship of imbalanced love, I knew early on that Mamabargains couldn't give me what I was giving to her—companionship, heart. It was a sexless, loveless marriage with her.

Being a 24/7 CEO took its toll. I thought we could go a year without hired help for the kids. We made it one month. By June, I had part time nanny Jenna who would watch our little guys and get our dinner started before she left. She enriched our lives, staying with our family for four years. She quickly grew into a full time employee and more. She became the daughter I never had, that I'd forever treasure.

But a nanny wasn't enough.

Soon after, I hired my first official non-contract employee, a friend of mine from a mommy group I was a part of. Her name was Renee (I'm not using her real name. That would just be mean. And I'm not mean).

At the time, it seemed like a good idea.

After firing her, we realized working with a friend was a terrible idea.

We learned that tracking a business phone is a must. Renee had been calling her out of state family every day, talking for hours on our business phone. Meanwhile, precious customers were complaining that they weren't getting responses to their queries for days. The family phone call minutes added up. There was no such thing as unlimited data back then. Talk about overhead! Those same customers who were so vital to the growth of our small but expanding business, the same ones that I'd answered the phone for at 2am were now being neglected. I had to put a stop to it.

I knew that the small things mattered. To a customer, being heard, and being responded to was a vital part of their Mamabargains.com experience. I wasn't asking Renee to respond to customers at 2am. I was paying her to respond to them during regular business hours, the same day they emailed. Basic guidelines for a very basic job.

Our first termination came sooner than I'd ever imagined. And it was harder than I ever thought possible. To make it simple, these were the only in person words she received from us:

"Renee, your services are no longer needed. Please return your keys, laptop, and the business phone within twenty-four hours."

I'd assumed it would be simple to keep personal and business separate.

But you know what happens when you assume, right?

You make an ass out of u and me...ass/u/me.

Renee was the first friend I'd lost since business inception. Our friendship was over—finished forever. It broke my heart. I knew it would be lonely at the top.

I'm not as cutthroat as I'd like, and because apparently I like repetition, I chose to replace Renee with...

Another friend!

The new girl kicked ass, though. Becca was the daughter of a good friend of ours. She babysat our oldest when he was an infant, so we knew her well. Our kids knew her well.

Becca was an integral part of our success, I'll be grateful to her forever for that.

I knew I'd have to toughen up to make Mamabargains a huge success. I'd already learned a few tough lessons—the first was that I'd have to put this business before myself. I knew that I needed to grow thick skin, that I'd be tired all of the time, but would need to always demonstrate high-level energy.

I recognized these things, and more, but suspected I wasn't going to be ready for what lay ahead—good or bad.

How could I ever prepare for such an unknown?

6. THE SINGLE-MINDED CEO

I was still on a low after the loss of Renee's friendship, which caused slight problems at first in the mommy group I was a part of. Apparently she felt uncomfortable hanging out with all the ladies from our moms group after she'd been fired.

Since Renee was now an ex-friend of the other moms too, I reluctantly shared with them all of the experiences we had with her and what led to the firing. Their ears were burning and they were dying to know what had happened. I was honest in answering their questions—brutally so. Renee had already been let go, and they knew what type of a person this girl was. 'Socially awkward' is what we called her. They understood and supported me, and then we talked shit about her every single ladies night for the next four years. I soon realized that what was connecting all of us was ridiculing this poor girl who simply lacked social skills. I'd gotten to know Renee on a different level. She was the casualty of me making the best decisions I could under the pressure of trying to be a friend, a mom, a wife, and a successful, responsible business owner.

I ignored it for years, the fact that I realized most of these girls I was spending free time with once a month, were just so one-dimensional. They really never wanted to get to know Renee, they just wanted someone to be the butt of their jokes. It made me sad. But I was a willing participant—guilty as charged. Even though the girl had taken advantage of me and of Mamabargains, and even though she was bat-shit crazy, I still felt bad.

I wondered when I would become the butt of moms' club jokes?

I wondered when they'd turn on me.

Not long. It sure didn't take long.

Choose your friends wisely, because when you become a success, everyone wants to be your pal. When you begin to fail, or have failed, the ones left standing by your side—those are the real friends. Those who will hear you out, listen to your side of the story, and pick you up when you've fallen—those are the priceless friends. And in return, you'd do the same for them.

Real friends, they sure are something, aren't they?

I was known as a work-o-holic to my family and friends. They didn't see me without my phone. Ever. I love technology. And when it didn't work? I loved to hate it. I couldn't unplug. I didn't want to put it down. A normal sleeping pattern eluded me in my obsession with impeccable customer and vendor service. I was at the beck and call of our email servers.

I'd post on social media 24/7. There was no end in sight. I was always available, feeling as if I was working harder than any other single person I've ever known in my life. I was not getting paid to do it either in those first years, and only a pittance for several years after that. It didn't bother me one bit...until it did.

I watched the world having fun all around me as I spent every waking moment dedicating everything I had to Mamabargains.

Several years after we launched, Stanford jumped into the pool on our first ever three-day vacation with his phone in his pocket. Yeah, the business phone. The one we used to communicate with everyone back in the 'real world'. This rare moment of spontaneous fun tanked the remainder of our unplugging from business time with our kids. We were supposed to be basking in the sun on the beach with our kids. Instead, I was consumed with finding Wi-Fi so I could check in with the office.

Go to the beach? Not a chance—too far from the Wi-Fi connection at the hotel. I spent most of the sunshine hours staring at the wall in the hotel lobby, being 'available' for my employees. It was easier to be a workaholic than live a healthy, well-balanced life. I sort of want to be on the winning team *and* be the captain. Is that *so* wrong?

Sometimes, yes. Yes it is.

I don't think it's reasonable to expect yourself to give 100% of your energy to your kids, your spouse, yourself *and* a business. Something has to give. In my experience, as an entrepreneur and a workaholic, which really is one in the same—what typically suffers is *you.*

Find a coping mechanism.

Some people work out. Fuck that. I had no energy to work out, no extra minute in each day. Some people enjoy the great outdoors, except there's no Wi-Fi in nature.

Yoga was too quiet. My brain couldn't stop or slow down doing yoga, even though I tried.

Some people draw. I'm not certain the doodles of my childhood would be the appropriate remedy, though.

Writing. There it is. I already carried a briefcase full of shit so didn't want to add a journal to the mix. Also, writing by hand takes longer than I had time for. My decision was to sit at the black keys in front of me, and type.

I decided to write myself an email. I'd discovered my coping mechanism—it was me.

September 15th, 2008

Jess,

It's California. Just look at that beach out there calling your name. You don't give a shit, though, because you'd rather find faces and shapes in the drywall mud on that ceiling above you. Oh look, there's a unicorn. Look out that fucking window. I dare you. See that white sand beach out there? What if it's not there tomorrow? Ignore the thirty-seven new emails in your inbox. Don't look.

Hey, you! Queen of people watchers. Check out that six-pack on that hottie down by the pool! Her husband isn't half bad, either! Dip your toes in the ocean and let it all melt away. I dare you.

Yours Truly, Me

I didn't even have to use the 'I'm on my period' excuse anymore to avoid sex. You could see it on my face, the dark circles that I carried around. You could see the wrinkles forming and the gray hairs popping up out of nowhere. The tone in my voice said that I was overly exhausted. Stressed out. I was so busy being busy, that I forgot how to get busy not being busy. I forgot me. I forgot Stanford and the kids.

Schedule a day *every week* for just you. Do whatever the fuck you want to do, but don't work. Don't be available for work. Go to the gym, go on a hike, stare at a wall, but don't stare at a screen. If you've ever been a new parent, you're familiar with the term 'over-stimulation.' Usually it's reserved to describe not stimulating your baby to the point that it causes sensory overload. Here are a few of its symptoms thanks to Google, as I chuckle to myself reading them: irritability, muscle tension, sleeplessness/fatigue, difficulty concentrating, over-excitability, avoids touching or being touched, 'shuts down' or refuses interactions with others.

I laugh now, because I was these and more. Every entrepreneur I know is these and more. In looking back, I can see that I don't really know anyone who'd willingly want to be those things. I have to learn to control it. I have to learn to take it down a notch—to take a step back.

The alternative...?

It's time for my pill.

Mari-hwwwanna. Maryjane. Pot. Dope. It doesn't do much for me. A joint Stanford and I smoked while in the Netherlands proved to be the only time that it 'did' anything to me. I was filled with smiles and giddy, gut busting laughter—the high kind.

It's little wonder I hadn't gone near drugs at any point in my schooling or young, impressionable years. During High School, my choices in ~~men~~ boys left a lot to be desired. In eleventh grade, I chose a guy named Jake, a poet by nature. I thought I'd finally found someone who would truly inspire me.

I found Jake in English class.

Jake was a talented writer. He was eloquent, romantic, and funny. He was exactly what my life needed—someone full of life. We dated a short time, until he stole a car on his way to school and crashed it into some poor old lady's house. He was on the run for the better part of that day until the cops caught up with and arrested him.

The entire school knew about it. The high school druggies were probably worried their dealer was going to be locked-up.

After the car theft, Jake's parents kicked him out and he moved in with his lovely grandma. He went from being a great student to almost overnight, a juvenile delinquent. From this moment forward, and with every other ensuing arrest (what, did you think I'd waste my time dating a *one time* offender?), I had the honor of being his one phone call from jail. I was the plain-Jane librarian-type and this whole bad-boy thing really terrified/thrilled me. I had the foresight to know it was heading down a nasty path and wasn't sure I wanted any part of Jake's dangerous nonsense.

I couldn't say no—because he needed me.

And don't we all need to be needed?

I realize now that I was attracted to the exciting personalities, to the 'projects' that I could sink my teeth into. He was my project, similar to my childhood businesses. Jake wasn't as easy to mold as the clay from my old neighborhood, though.

But before the revelation I just *knew* I could change him. I'd focus my energies on helping Jake instead of looking at myself in the mirror and improving *me*.

What kind of an idiot am I? I was once smart. I'm still smart, only book smart, not street smart. Not yet, anyway.

I dated Jake, my wordsmith poet turned tortuous druggie boyfriend off and on for five years. Even though he was the one who was always high—out of it, much of it's a blur to me. We lived in about six different rental apartments and houses in and around the Tacoma, Washington area. Yeah, the aroma of Tacoma—*that* place.

Jake abused me often. He not only punched me, he verbally, and emotionally abused me. He raped my mind and soul, leaving me to grieve its loss. The abuse was off and on, just as our relationship was. Between apartments, his grandmother's spare bedroom, my parents' family room, and small rental homes, the places we lived always seemed about as temporary as our life together. They changed as often as whatever his current drug of choice was. I was the enabler that needed the distraction in my life.

And there were times when he said he'd changed.

"Jess, I'm a changed man," he'd say, surprising me with a bouquet of handpicked daisies—my favorite. "Baby, I love you, I'm going to show you every day just how much." Promises broken and repeated, apologies and daisies became more frequent.

He'd go through rehab, kick the drugs and alcohol and then he'd be my wonderful poet again for a few months. During the entire relationship, I endured beatings, both physical and verbal.

Lather, rinse and repeat.

I watched my self-worth deteriorate until I sank into a deep depression. I tried, but continually failed, to apply my misguided energies on the enemy before me. That enemy was the person I saw in the mirror every morning. I was against myself in every sense. I hated *me*. I hated what I'd become but couldn't stand who I once was.

I knew it was a matter of when, not if, I'd be found dead in a gutter somewhere.

I called the police on Jake regularly. I spoke to his probation officers more often than I visited or spoke to my own family. No doubt worried that I'd leave him if anyone had the chance to talk sense into me, Jake forbade me to visit or speak to my family.

Little Miss Drug Free spent an inordinate amount of time watching large drug deals 'going down'. Never once in all of those years did I ever touch the product. My first hit of weed would come many years later, post Jake the druggie.

Drugs revolted me.

I loathed the cat piss smell of methamphetamines. The yellowish powder began as a crystal before it was crushed. I hate that I have that visual in my head and remember the smell, even after all these years. The sound of snorting was far more repellant than the worst flu symptoms or food poisoning you could imagine. I couldn't stomach it. It nauseated me, leaving me feeling dirty after I witnessed it. Drugs gave me a horrific sensory overload of smells, sounds and sights.

I'd spend time with Jake in broke-down houses with trashy people, and had no idea why. It was exciting for a while, a welcome change from my day-to-day school, work, library, work, sleep, then school, library, work, work, and more sleep.

I have never been one to tolerate a monotonous routine. I need change. I need adventure and healthy chaos. The Jake era was no exception, minus the healthy part.

The only up side was that I used the craptastic experience of watching drug deals go down to learn about the inner workings of entrepreneurship.

Even though there was a great margin on drugs, it was fairly obvious to me that Jake's business model had one major issue—the CEO of Jake Pharmaceuticals Inc. was smoking, snorting, drinking and shooting up all the profits, plus some. The deadbeat was selling thousands of dollars of product a week, but hadn't paid his portion of rent in months. I managed to turn a reprehensible situation into a business lesson. I guess it's in my DNA.

I taught Jake, the former poet, later turned loser-drug dealer how to take the profit and turn it into more products—reinvesting back into his business venture.

"Just take at least half of your profit and put it aside, when a good deal comes your way, you've got the cash stashed" I advised, not really understanding the impact his addiction could have on the business plan, no matter how attractive.

Jake the CEO wasn't going to win any 'greatest business' awards, but the reinvestment plan actually worked while the only drug he was consuming was marijuana. Once the alcohol crept back into the picture, all of my professional advice went right out the window. The guy was desperate for his next high, and nothing else mattered to him.

And then, as if life wasn't interesting enough, at age twenty and several years into our light switch courtship, I found out I was pregnant with the spawn of Satan.

I should have been overjoyed, but considering my circumstances, it was the single worst news I'd ever received. A life is value. I valued this life inside of me. All I could imagine, though, was bringing a child into the world with *him* as a father. How would a child turn out with his *genes*?

We'd used protection. We *always* used protection.

I dreaded telling my parents I was pregnant. When I told them, I was only eight weeks along and they were naturally terrified for me.

"You're not serious, Squirt, are you?" were my dad's words. At least he used the nickname he gave me when I was just a few years old. His affections eased my tension. My mom leveled a stern stare. No words, just the long look. And it was louder than any words she could've yelled. Because I knew that look defined her deep love for me, her oldest child.

My youngest brother went to a thrift store and bought a baby blanket, over the moon to have a new addition to our family. He couldn't wait to be an uncle.

You know what you have to do.

Judge me if you will, but it's my body, my right, my life, and my decision. There really was no other option.

I aborted the life inside. I'd have to live with the decision without a moment's regret in the incredibly difficult choice. I knew it would shape me and what type of mother I'd eventually become someday.

Any misgivings on my part were soon put to rest when the would've been father of my could've been child kicked our dog almost to death. She was guilty of the minor transgression of chewing one of Jake's golf balls to pieces—because he'd left it out.

Bringing a child anywhere near his violence and madness? I finally had absolute closure. The decision was sealed with each moment of Jake's rage I'd witnessed over the years, with each minute I spent at the emergency vet clinic explaining why our dog had broken ribs. With every bump and bruise on my own body, I saved the life of my unborn child.

The disappointment on my baby brothers' face when he learned that I was no longer pregnant is another long look that I'll never forget.

Thank goodness as women, we have the right to choose what's best for ourselves, for our *own* bodies.

Afterwards, I placed a single daisy on an empty plot at the local cemetery. I cried until I had no more tears to give. And then I walked away from that cemetery, never to return again.

It's amazing, but even after that, I still couldn't leave Jake. We spent twelve months living in a dump in the gang-ridden area of Hilltop in Tacoma, Washington. Hilltop? Sounds quite nice. Nope. Picture a place similar to hell, awash with drugs, murders, and a crime rate that would put prison itself to shame. Hilltop was *not* a safe place for me.

I worked at a credit union at the time, and I drove with an unregistered gun under my seat. Matter of fact, I later discovered that the gun was stolen from Jake's grandpa. When I told his grandmother that he'd stolen the gun from his grandfather, she told me to keep it with me at all times for safety. So I did as she asked. There were occasions when he beat me so badly that I came close to actually using it.

In our lovely, white-picket, homely (in my dreams) neighborhood (where gunfire was the nightly fixture) three nine-year-olds stood on the corner and sold drugs. They lived a block away, and instead of attending school, they were drug hustlers, selling crack. Dime bags and eight balls of white powder, and—well, not sure if I got the street lingo right, but equally certain the details didn't really matter, because these were *kids*. One of them supposedly murdered his sister when he was six. That was the 'word on the street'. I'd barely learned the art of entrepreneurship selling lemonade and offering gymnastics camp by the age of nine. Murder? No thanks. Drugs at age nine? I didn't smoke my first joint until I was well into my twenties!

And speaking of 'on the street'—we were surrounded by these wonderful citizens—real contributors to our lovely community. One neighbor had just been released from prison for the rape and murder of two teenage girls. And the guy just three houses down? He was a serial arsonist out on work release.

Jake thought it was hilarious when he picked up a weight set and bench from a neighborhood garage sale. He was *the* white trash cliché as he put on his whitest 'wife-beater' tank top and sat out in the front yard bench-pressing double my weight, with all of our wonderful spectating criminal neighbors cheering him on.

He was the white guy who considered himself a 'brotha'. He would say, "I'm a black man in a skinny, white body," and in my mind, I'd think, *No. You're actually just a skinny, white tweeker asshole. Fucking wannabe.*

I lost count of the times I stared at my hated self in the mirror thinking, *For fuck's sakes, Jessica, what the hell are you still doing with this psycho?*

One of my most charming memories was when Jake was acting more foolish than normal. He was even more abrasive, and physically aggressive than I'd ever seen him.

"What are you on this time, Jake?"

"I'm a crack head, baby. I'm smoking cigarettes dipped in embalming fluid with the neighbor," he replied.

What. The. Actual. *FUCK.*

Seriously?

Who comes up with this stuff? Cigarettes dipped in embalming fluid? Is he out of his goddamn gourd? I could think it, but never say it aloud.

So, for years I stayed, and hated that reflection in the mirror every time I saw it. In the end, I just stopped looking. We broke up, we got back together, I left him, we got back together, and we broke up again.

Battered person syndrome, Stockholm syndrome, whatever you want to label it, I felt trapped in an endless cycle of absolute nonsense.

I watched him sell and use angel dust, marijuana, mushrooms, coke, methamphetamines, pills—anything he could get his hands on, including the aforementioned super-classy cigarettes dipped in the liquid used to preserve fucking corpses. But the very worst drug of all, no contest was alcohol. The man-child was a die-hard alcoholic.

The drug that provided him with all the ammunition he needed to throw punch and kick after punch and kick, while at the same time verbally assaulting anyone who stepped into his path. And most of the time, Jessica was the lucky one in his path.

I was terrified of him, but I wanted to love him for the poet I first met, when he was responsible (ish), smart, funny and kind. Those days were gone. I was a fool to believe otherwise.

Leaving Jake is one of my favorite, life-altering memories, because it's when I grew the hell up. I have no idea what came over me or why the thought of leaving him finally, after five years with this piece of work, became real and actionable. What prompted me to the realization that this man would eventually kill me if I didn't get out?

When I put my mind to something...

I called the moving company, rented a trailer and quit my job in one single morning. The landlord in the home we rented more than understood—he knew I was in an abusive situation and he was proud of me for leaving. I phoned my one and only acquaintance in Utah and asked her if she'd fly up and drive back down to Utah with me. Amanda and I weren't particularly close, but we'd met when we were nannies in New York many years before. She agreed to help.

Utah?

I knew Jake wouldn't think to look for me in Mormon country. So that was it. Amanda flew out that afternoon, looking for an adventure, and I had enough funds in my bank account to pay for the drive down to Salt Lake City and get into an apartment. It was 2001 and the Olympics were coming to Salt Lake City only a few months later, it would be easy to find work in that economy.

Later that afternoon, I picked Amanda up from the airport, stopping on my way 'home' to drop the moving trailer in the Church parking lot down the road. It was a surprise for already drunk Jake to see her, but I felt safer with Amanda backing me up. The plan was to take Jake clubbing—that way he'd get good and drunk, do his usual and pass out. We'd grab my few possessions and get the hell out of Dodge as soon as he was in dreamland.

The plan was working perfectly, until it wasn't...

Jake invited along his friend, Gerome, to make a foursome. Jake drank himself into obliteration. When we returned to our house later, more than hell broke loose. Did I really think the escape plan was going to be that easy?

Jake grabbed a gallon of bottom-shelf whiskey that he'd hidden in the garage, and proceeded to guzzle *every last drop*. I didn't know in those moments how he was able to sidestep the grips of death, but I really wished he wouldn't have because not long after his impressive two-minute mouth grip on the bottle, the shit hit the proverbial fan.

With a tank full of cheap booze, Jake turned nasty. He began punching me. First my stomach, then in my arm, next, on my back. He started kicking me and pushing me.

He yelled, "GO GET ME MORE ALCOHOL, BITCH!"

And then, "YOU'RE A PUSSY!" when the tears came rolling down my face.

Over and over again he told me, "I HATE YOU".

He screamed it in my face, so close his spit was filling my eyes and tear-stained cheeks, "I. FUCKING. HATE. YOUR. UGLY. FACE."

Leave. You have to leave now.

Every bruise, every ounce of energy Jake put into harming me, I took another step away from him and into another life—my new life. He had no idea I was leaving him. The trouble was, because of Jake's verbal and physical beatings, I wasn't even sure I'd be alive to make the escape. I feared for my life.

But then...a miracle happened.

His drunk-ass friend, Gerome, who'd never stood up to Jake, even though he'd been witness to the multiple beatings I suffered over the years, finally manned up. He stood up higher than I ever thought someone could stand up for me.

Gerome's blows were stronger than those of Jake's. They were firm, his words resolute.

"Don't ever touch Jessica again. Don't ever touch another girl ever again. When I'm done with you, you won't even be able to beat off, much less hurt anyone!"

As soon as we saw them throwing punches at each other, Amanda and I made our escape. The fight was so violent I truly believed we'd be witness to murder if we stayed.

Amanda and I fled the house, calling the police on our way out the door. We headed straight for the Church parking lot to get the trailer.

We were gone only twenty minutes, but we knew something was terribly wrong. Cop cars were screaming past. We lost count of how many, and there were several more in the driveway when we arrived.

We should've just kept going, but I had to see what the aftermath looked like. I wanted to see Gerome triumphant. I wanted to see a body bag. I swear, I've never wished anyone dead in my life, but I wished that Jake could never harm anyone ever again.

Damn, was I ever *disappointed*.

Jake *did* get what was coming to him. Gerome had beaten him within an inch of his life. His shoulder was broken, his elbow bent in a direction that couldn't be considered anything less than excruciating. It was swollen to the size of two baseballs. Blood from his ear canal was draining from his head. That can't be good, right?

In fact, there was more blood than I'd ever seen in my life. Jake's face was nearly unrecognizable, as if he'd just been through a meat grinder. He was lying flat, helpless on his back while Gerome stood in the corner answering a barrage of questions from several officers.

Upon arrival, the officers wanting to piece together the events of the evening immediately questioned us. We helped as best as we could, but they could see I was physically hurt by him as well. A bruise on my right cheek, and a look in my eyes that begged, *this is my escape from the monster, please let me leave in peace.*

The paramedics came in and wheeled the asshole away. Gerome was loaded into a police cruiser. Away they went. The house was quiet, Jake's blood coated the floor.

I called his grandmother to let her know what was going on, and that I was out—escape was now or never. I was sad to be leaving her to deal with the aftermath, but had to stick to my plan.

We finished packing up the moving trailer. Freedom was so close I could almost taste it.

Not so fast, Jess.

"Please come to the hospital to say goodbye to Jake". His grandma pleaded with me.

She wanted me to see him one last time, at his lowest, to carry with me the memory of him handcuffed to a hospital bed, close to losing his sorry excuse for a life.

She also wanted Jake to know that I was leaving, and for him to have a chance to say goodbye to me. Of course I didn't think he deserved it, but she did, and this sweet, kind woman, who cared for Jake more than she should have, was very persuasive.

I obliged. It was good to see Jake at his lowest. He was in a cast with his face pulverized and already turning multiple shades of lobster and plum. To be there when he was the completely powerless one, the coward, the pussy, knowing that this was the way I'd get to remember him—that was my moment of triumph.

Even today, the nurse's words sends chills down my spine. The truth was finally out. What he'd done to himself that night, why the gallon of whiskey that he downed didn't kill him absolutely baffled me.

"He's high out of his mind. We found *multiple* different drugs in his system, including coke *and* methamphetamines," the Nurse explained in a calm voice. "Quite frankly, if he hadn't taken the drugs, he'd be dead right now."

I gave his grandma one last hug, and told her where I was going before turning and walking away from that broken bastard forever. Telling her where I was going was a major mistake, because I ended up spending the next two years in Utah scared out of my wits.

It began with dead roses on the hood of my car, and then visits to my work place from 'a stranger who's tall with dark hair, claiming to be your brother,' according to colleagues as I hid in the supply closet. I could tell that they were being polite about my 'brother' because they were actually frightened, only a few of them knowing the life I'd escaped in Washington.

Many nights I'd hide under the covers in my studio apartment while someone banged forcibly on the door outside. The terror campaign lasted for weeks, and just when I thought I'd have to go on the run again, it suddenly ceased.

The unimaginable pain he caused me was what catapulted me into a new life. It's made me a smarter, resilient, more aware individual. It gave me the opportunity to have experiences in life that others could only read about in a book.

I wanted more for myself than bruises, scratches and emotional abuse. I wanted more than drug profits from my addict and dealer of a boyfriend. You've got to experience the dark before you can appreciate the light.

Don't let the shit times define you.

This was the moment of my rebirth.

Those few vendors that laughed at our idea when we pitched them in the beginning, I never forgot them. I have a notebook with their names. The notebook should serve as inspiration to ignore the haters and push on. Or to exact revenge. Your choice.

Not everyone loved the concept of Mamabargains.

Competition came in all forms.

There was the owner of a cute line of little girls clothing. His name was Bill. He laughed—literally *out loud*—when I said I'd need to purchase his clothing at least 75% off his retail price point. After he was done with his maniacal, deflating bout of mirth, he said, "Um, yeah. Good luck with your crappy business idea. *No one* will sell to you at those margins. I hope you enjoy failure."

Initially humiliated and embarrassed, I took Bill's sarcasm and laughter as a challenge and an important lesson. The fact is, even Steve Jobs and John at Backcountry would've encountered naysayers, and I wanted to be more like them than Bill the jackass with the little girls clothing line.

And guess what? Two years after our initial conversation, naysaying Bill tried to launch his own deal site. It lasted exactly two days.

It was oddly refreshing to sit back and watch his previous negative intentions disintegrate because apparently our 'crappy business' idea was one he wished he'd thought of himself. Usually when people put you down, it's a reflection of their own lack of self-confidence.

Remember when I mentioned that we bought just one domain name, Mamabargains.com, and how proud I was back in those first moments of business ownership? I thought that buying a single name meant I was single-minded, focused—confident in the concept, the company and our journey.

In reality, it meant I'd made my first newbie mistake. I hadn't learned that in business, you must protect yourself. This is all encompassing—it means domain names, copyrights, patents and/or trademarks. You'd be foolish to believe that there are only well-intentioned people in this universe. There aren't (Hi Bill!). Buying just the one name showed my business naiveté.

I soon found out why.

A few days before the Mamabargains site went live, a good friend of mine called, "Jess, I can't believe your company launched and you didn't even tell me!" she said, clearly annoyed with me for not telling her we'd launched already.

I was so crazy-busy with the launch details that I was mentally unprepared for this dirty game of pool so early on.

"Huh?"

"Yeah, I got the email about your new deal site 'Babysteals'. I guess I should say congrats!"

"No. You definitely should *not* say that."

"What? Why? I think your site looks great! I already made a purchase!"

"No! No, you didn't! That's not my site."

After a little research, it appeared that yes, there *was* another mommy deal site, and yes, they were first into the market.

Baby steals had their domain name long before we did, I'll give them that. And that's about all we knew of our archrival in that early stage. We had no clue who the owners were, where they came from, or how it was possible that they launched with exactly the same business model—only weeks from our own launch date. The very business model, geared toward the mommy market, the one we'd shared only a week earlier with the owner of Backcountry.com.

How could this happen?

Hang on just a minute!

It was too much of a coincidence.

After some minor digging, I discovered that the number one investor at this new company had worked as the Online Media Manager for Backcountry. Maybe he'd read the business plan we'd left on John's desk? Did they know that we'd reached out to John and then decided to jump into launching at the speed of light so they could beat us to the punch? John was always above reproach, so was this an unintentional or—eek—intentional leak? We've never discovered the absolute truth, but it was a nasty introduction to the competitive nature of online business. From this rude awakening on, we were constantly on our toes, protecting ourselves.

At first, dealing with competition, you think of the old saying 'keep your friends close, and your enemies closer.' Unfortunately, you soon realize that it's a hell of a lot harder than you could ever imagine. I had to be certain Babysteals was our only competitor at launch.

Now, obviously Mamabargains was born from Backcountry's original concept, aimed at an entirely different demographic. To fight off this new threat, we'd have to be bigger—in the figurative form, hopefully in the literal form as well. Yes—we'd treat competition as flattery in its most sincere form. That philosophy works great, until things get cutthroat—be prepared if it does.

It sure didn't take long.

A few weeks after the launch of Mamabargains, one of our customers emailed to let us know that she was really confused. When she typed Mamabargains into her web address bar, she'd forgotten the 's' at the end of the word. As a result, she ended up landing on a website called, you guessed it—Babysteals.com. Those smart shitheads.

Our competitor had very cannily purchased the domain name Mamabargain.com, and directed *our* traffic from the Mamabargain.com domain over to their own website. This meant that every time a customer forgot to type the 's' on the word Mamabargains, they'd go straight to our competition!

I hated them, whoever they were. I hated them for being so fucking genius.

I had to embrace their brilliance, jealous it wasn't from my own playbook. Had I come up with something so clever myself, though, I'm not convinced I'd have had the balls to act upon it. Because—karma.

I had no experience in the domain name industry—but they clearly did. Whoever they were. I didn't know that buying bulk domain names would protect my company and its brand—but *they sure did*. We should have bought mamabargain.com, mamabargains.com, mamabargin.com— any variation or possible misspelling of our name.

I'd been outmaneuvered and my only recourse was legal. I was in over my head. This misstep of ours could tank us before we'd even started.

At this point in the game of dirty pool, (that we were losing) I brought in a trademark attorney. And I chose a shark. She sent cease and desist letters to Babysteals accusing them of 'domain name confusion'. After she explained what it was, she suggested we fight fire with fire. So I quickly bought infantsdeals.com. It sounded better than Babysteals anyway, right? It sounded almost like the same name, with less of an emphasis on the stealing of infants, which I'd always thought was weird...but I digress. Then I bought Infantsdeals, Mamasteals, Infantseals and a slew of others that I thought they'd potentially want—maybe not then, but someday.

The tactic worked.

We negotiated a deal where they'd turn over the singular Mamabargain domain, and in exchange we'd give them Infantsdeals. It was straight trade that would haunt me for the following six years. They didn't need to know I owned the other ones. Those others I held onto—just in case.

It was only the first skirmish in the ongoing tempestuous relationship with our number one competitor. Mamabargains vs. Babysteals lasted into our dying business breaths. It was frustrating, confusing and infuriating. It also kept us on our toes every single hour of every single day.

The next step for me in the mom deal site smack down was to put a face to the name.

"Know thine enemy." That's also what they say, right?

I met with the owner of Babysteals, my arch nemesis, for lunch one afternoon. You know, neutral territory. I needed to see the monster that was trying to wipe me off the face of the Internet, and I seriously expected a witch to fly into the restaurant on her broomstick. But, the witch who'd been trying to kill my business actually turned out to be a very pretty former model.

She used to work in marketing for our local news station. Ugh. She's a mom too. Great. She was fit, slender, blonde, and just an ounce better than me in every single way. She was a perfect match for the job of running her company, and ruining mine. Dammit!

Why'd she have to be so damn perfect? She breathed life into my own insecurities.

My ulterior motive was that a friendly lunch and future relationship would hopefully make ~~witchlady~~ my lovely competitor slightly less cutthroat. I mean, how could she not love the charming mom, slightly less fit, slightly less slender, brunette sub-par *me* sitting across the table?

We chatted about our kids, our husbands, and bonded over salad. We talked about our previous business experience. She shared her extensive list of credentials, and I changed the subject. She intimidated me with her background and financial backers. The rumor mill circulating in the business world was that Babysteals started with several million in investments (more than one vendor shared this little tidbit with us). Who knew if it was authentic information or not, all I knew was that we were the same age, but this woman had experience and money. Me? I had street smarts and $12 in my checking account.

When the check arrived, I said with a smile worth a million board game bucks, "I'll get it."

"Oh, no, that's okay, I'll put it on the business card," she offered.

"I'll get it next time, then," I gallantly offered, knowing full well there probably wouldn't be a next time.

It appears I still owe you a lunch, lovely lady.

If I were an idiot, I'd have felt as if the face-to-face lunch had worked. But since I'm smarter than I appear, I knew she was on her toes as much as I was. Keeping a peripheral eye on our competition became part of the job. Over the years, we kept in touch, a quick text here or there. At least we were on the same page after both having the same ulterior motive for the lunch in that first year.

What are they doing and can we do it better? What products are they selling? Can we sell them cheaper? How many babies has Babysteals stolen? Kidding, you get the picture.

We knew we were capable of doing some things better than our rival, but would it be enough? Could we outwit, out-sell and out-service them, winning over the largest shopping demographic that ever existed? The mom demographic. You win these types of customers over and you can rule the retail world. The year before our launch, according to Entrepreneur online magazine[1], the mommy market was worth over 1.6 *trillion* dollars. That's a demographic worth targeting.

When the big dogs launched, the big huge deal sites like Zulily and Groupon (that have essentially taken over the world), Mamabargains vowed to take em' all down. We may have failed, but we tried. Hell, there's even Amazon Mom now. They launched two years after Mamabargains' launch. Jeff? Maybe you should have called it Momazon. You're welcome. Just credit me for the name invention, would ya?

The reality is, even successful companies doing six figures cannot compete with a larger competitor doing over one *billion* a year. Not even Babysteals. Misery loves company. I reveled in the fact that they too, were hurt, even a bit, by the largest mom deal site to launch. Zulily.com. Damn you, Darrell Cravens.

But all of this was just another lesson for me. Healthy competition is vital for the scalability of business. If you have any type of expansion in mind, keep a healthy relationship with the competition. Cheer for them. I'm still cheering for the owner today, long after Mamabargains closed. It feels like the right thing to do, even though she is fit, slender, blonde, perfect, and probably doesn't need a cheerleader.

But Babysteals wasn't our only competitor. There were scads of copycats, too.

There was the site that right-clicked on the Mamabargains' home page and stole the source code of our website. Then they launched a deal site called Llamabargains. It looked identical to Mamabargains, except our pregnant little stick-mama icon on our home page, became—a llama. The colors were even the same. It was a carbon copy down to the font, the wording—all of it—of Mamabargains. Even their 'about us' page...all of our website content that I'd written myself, they copied. Llamabargains, huh? Were they offering some zoo deals or something? Speaking of zoos—what an asinine name.

This world was so new to me. I couldn't believe the audacity. I was just livid, but also, really offended. It's one thing to take the concept and alter it slightly to fit your own model, but it's another thing entirely to completely rip-off our entire website. Keep in mind, our site was customized, there were no plug-in, ready-made features. This website of ours was created *by us*, from the ground up, by trial and error, customer feedback, sweat and tears, and cold hard cash from the Jessica and Stanford Singer bank.

It was back to our shark attorney who contacted the Llamabargains fools and sent them cease and desist letters. For weeks we waited, checking their site multiple times a day, watching for the rip-off Llamas to change their plagiarized site.

Two weeks later, our lovely attorney succeeded in the copycat site shutdown. Their site would be forever gone and forever forgotten. Except me, I'll never forget. I'll give them that.

There were others, too, like Ohbabymamabargains and Omamabargains. These rip-offs lasted less than twenty-four hours. There wasn't room for any more competitors. Customers became our advocates, reporting copycats became their mission—shutting them down before they had a chance to do too much damage to our bottom-line, one of our primary objectives.

Then there was the Organicbabybargains who came at us from a different, slightly shadier angle. They attempted to steal every vendor that worked exclusively with Mamabargains. They lasted just over a year. There was also Mamabargainz, (Zzzz), and who could forget the Mombargin site which launched their website not realizing they'd spelled the word 'bargain' incorrectly. Curiously, mothers never flocked to them, and they, too, closed within days.

There was a reason we worked so closely with our vendors, and why many were un-poachable and loyal. Mamabargains took care of our friends. We nurtured those relationships with our vendors and helped their brands grow right up until the end. We took great pride in marketing their products to our customers. I worked with many of them one-on-one, and many of our suppliers still call or text to check in—years after we closed. There are even those vendors that we left at the very end not being able to pay. Those ones—they are the ones that I will forever be not just grateful for, but sorry to as well. Most of them forgave us, because maybe they'd been there themselves. I'm so sorry we couldn't pay you.

Some competition came from unlikely places. There was the cousin who launched her own deal site. In the process, she called many of our vendors, telling them, "Jessica told me to call you. She said you'd work with me on my deal site as well."

Did she not think that those vendors would contact me and ask me if I was crazy enough to send a competitor their way?

The backstabbing business-play pretty much ended disastrously for cousin Liar-Liar Pants on Fire, because I bypassed the shark attorney, and sent in the big gun—Stanford. One phone call ended what she'd started. Not certain, but her decision making abilities may have contributed to the demise of her relationship with our family, as well as her marriage.

Even though Babysteals isn't my competitor anymore, I think back to that first time we met, how intimidated I felt. I attribute some of our small successes in part to my unwillingness to settle for second best. I wanted Mamabargains to be number one. Sometimes, though, winning is accepting that you didn't finish in first place, but that you tried your hardest in the race for second.

Not long after exchanging ceremonial pleasantries over salads during that first meeting with the owner of Babysteals, the tides would turn. Mamabargains would one-up them. We'd do something so brazen, so bold, that it would mark the time in our professional careers that we were at our most successful. It would become a chapter in our Mamabargains story that wouldn't soon be forgotten.

It was the moment, long before it was even a 'thing', that Mamabargains went 'viral'.

---

[1] http://www.entrepreneur.com/article/176978

Children are a product of their environment. I'm no exception. My spirited approach to business and the world as I see it directly correlates to my teenage years—the ones that followed me well into my adult years.

Those years were filled with failures, lessons I later learned to turn into successes.

He went from normal loving Dad, to out of this world bonkers in what seemed like the space of three days. I was only eleven.

I never realized the cause Dad's snap, until our entire family sat around chatting on Christmas Eve 2010.

Junior High. Life was just perfect—average. Dad was the man who'd work on his old '64 Chevy truck, kicking the wheel, calling it a 'stupid bitch' when 'she' wouldn't work. He usually had a beer in his hand. I'd take a rare sip, forever solidifying my distaste for cheap, piss beer.

Dad was a cool guy.

He built me that old balance beam for my summer gymnastics camp—the one I hosted in my backyard for all the neighbor kids. Constructed out of railroad ties and shag carpet, that balance beam represented my childhood (and one of my first entrepreneurial ventures.). Dad built that beam with love.

Our family hosted the local water fights. All the neighbors would hook up their hoses and the kids would run from yard to yard while the parents tried to douse them. See, trailer park living wasn't half bad at all!

Dad generously coached tee ball and softball for his three kids, too.

We had whipped cream fights in our dining room (Mom started it!), and all in all, it was a *great, adventure filled* childhood.

We camped out, sometimes just in our backyards, sometimes alongside any number of the local Washington lakes we loved visiting. We started fires in the woods (sorry about that, Graham Fire Department!), built forts, played on the gigantic tree swing Dad built, collected slugs and garter snakes in mom's laundry baskets (to her dismay), and played from sunup until sundown on our BMX bikes.

Then we moved.

We moved to a nicer neighborhood in a nearby town, where I started the sixth grade. It marked the fifth elementary school I'd attended. One would become overcrowded, so they'd reassign the students and move them to a new school. Physically moving homes and going to a different school felt like nothing new to our family.

But this time was different. Moving to a different town meant the beginning of major change for our family of five.

Dad was (and still is) a kind man. Unlike one (if not more) of his children (me), he was non-judgmental, truly loving and caring for everyone around him. He possessed a spirit and life about him that I looked up to and admired. He was 'spiritual', but in his own unique un-churchy way. Dad never talked about God, or Jesus, 'goddamn it' was a regularly heard slip of tongue on his part. Religion was definitely not a part of my younger years.

All that changed with 'the illness.'

The illness not only took over Dad, but it invaded our lives as well. Dad's illness took hold, testing our entire family's sanity—striking so suddenly without a known cause or *cure*. One day he was Dad. Snap. The next—Dad was gone.

It started fast, taking hold, seemingly coming from nowhere.

Could Dad die from this?

Is it contagious—hereditary?

Can you catch crazy?

It began with Dad wanting us to attend Church. Fine. People go to Church, even some people who say 'goddamnit', presumably. Dad *insisted* we attend Church, not just occasionally, but *demanded* every single one of us attend every single Sunday.

To some, that might seem normal. But for my beer-drinking, cursing, hilarious dad who'd never before even mentioned Church, it was shockingly out of character. Out of the blue, he demanded that we all do this Church thing every Sunday.

Something was definitely wrong, because not long after the insistence of Church attendance, Dad thought he was Jesus.

The day before, he said he was a prophet of God.

There were things that I later discovered were happening behind the scenes, but this was the view from an eleven-year-old girl's perspective, and from down there, my fun-loving dad suddenly didn't seem to love fun anymore.

Next came the praying, the bible reading, and, not every so often—we're talking *constant* praying and bible reading.

He went from being engaged with his kids, to reading the Bible, every day, non-stop. There were times I'd see him read the same chapter multiple times over again. I'd sit there, doing my homework, wishing I could interrupt him. Even just for a brief moment of paternal guidance with my damn Math. I didn't mumble so much as a word, though, fearing admonishment for my lack of biblical enthusiasm and respect.

I hated the damn thing. It represented negativity in my life, a huge obstruction between my dad, and his family. He didn't refer to me as 'Squirt' anymore. A childhood nickname that made me smile when he said it. It made me feel extra special. He just called me Jess-i-ca—enunciating each syllable as I was in trouble for something.

His eyes looked phony. Like glass. Glazed over with nothingness behind them.

Dad was gone. And, unfortunately, that was just the beginning. Soon after, my dad got *real*, consumed by religion.

Bible studies at the local Church, mission trips, youth group, and any and all activities that the Church held were my fate. When I say 'the Church' I'm actually referring to more than one because we went to about seven different Churches while we lived in the same small town in Washington. With my record of five different elementary schools, this was something I could adjust to.

We didn't leave the Churches willingly or quietly. We were kicked out of them. Expelled from Church! And not for being sinners—we were expelled from Church for being the opposite. They booted us out for being *too enthusiastic*.

Sometimes Dad would stand up in the middle of the sermon and loudly profess his love for Jesus Christ. Okay, fine, maybe his timing wasn't perfect. Other times, Dad spoke in tongues. I mean, the official term the pastor used was speaking in tongues, but to me, it all sounded like he was trying to speak without a tongue. Maybe he was taking French on the side? Who was I to judge?

"Speaking in tongues is disruptive to the other members of the Church, Sir," one Pastor told him.

"I don't appreciate you interrupting my Sermon for your own personal gain!" said another one.

Screw the fact that my dad gave money generously every Sunday to every Church we ever attended. In effect, we were 'paying customers'. Plus, if any of these men of God had looked closely and sympathetically, they'd have noticed that we most definitely needed guidance and sympathy.

Instead, these Churches made fun of us, taunting my dad over his excessive Bible reading, ridiculing Dad's Jesus obsession.

"He doesn't even know what that passage really means," I overheard one parishioner behind us saying to his wife. These Churches *judged* us. Nazarene, Episcopal, Baptist, non-denominational Christian, Lutheran, Presbyterian—they all kicked us out or shunned us in a very un-Christian-like way. Instead of turning their cheeks, they kicked our butts to the curbs they came from.

Adding insult to injury, the backlash and jokes at school were plentiful. After being kicked out on a Sunday, I dreaded school on Monday. There was always someone new to make fun of me for my dad's latest episode in God's house. Nowadays, they'd call that bullying, but back then, I just took it. I was scoffed at, spat at, laughed at, pointed at, and picked-on through the last part of Junior High and much of High school. Small towns will talk. Odd how I was exhibiting the most Christian-like turns the cheek the other way attitude, while the other church-going goody-goody folk weren't practicing what was being preached.

Acceptance, people.

Mom did her thing and went to work, socializing with only her fellow co-workers and a few family members and family friends who knew of the trouble Dad was going through. I mingled with almost no one.

My Health teacher, Mrs. Maxfield, taught me to 'Choose the Highest Good', to always do what was best for me. I was the only student she bought a graduation gift for—a keychain engraved with the initials CTHG, a daily reminder to look after myself. The other ear and protector was my English teacher. RIP Mr. Culver, I still miss our talks. He encouraged me to write it all down, to get it all out and to breathe. He was there to offer me a hug the day I was awarded the Alumni scholarship my senior year in High School and noticed my parents weren't there. I told Mom, but she had to work. Dad was probably in the mental institution at the time. My best friend's mom came to support me. I was spending a lot of time at their house, because there was always something weird going on at mine, and her being there meant the world to me.

I had a picture of Jesus in my room that I picked up for $3 at a garage sale. It was gorgeous. If I had to guess what Jesus looked like, he might as well be hot, especially if he was going to be hanging on my bedroom wall, staring at me while I slept every night, right?

My personal Jesus sported flowy beach-wavy hair, flawless skin, and eyelashes the envy of every woman alive. He was Jesus DiCaprio. Sorry Leonardo, Jesus was hotter than you. He also kind of reminded me of an older, more mature version of Joey, my New Kids on the Block crush, just with long hair. The non-Messiah real Joey adorned the opposite wall, so I had two handsomes looking down on me while I slept.

Unfortunately, my father took a shine to my handsome Jesus as well, and my bedroom became a place of pilgrimage. He'd often turn-up in the middle of the night to pray to Handsome Jesus of Jessica's Wall. I couldn't hear what he was praying about, or why, but clearly he needed this special time with the big guy. I pretended to be asleep, a sad attempt to ignore the bizarre scene of Dad kneeling on my floor in what appeared to be his bathrobe and a pair of tighty-whities. A grown man kneeling in my lavender painted room, talking earnestly to Jesus, amongst the dirty clothes, love letters and teen magazines. Apart from Joey watching from the adjacent wall, the lines of dark teenage angst filled poetry I'd written in permanent marker on my floor length mirror stared at Dad, begging him for guidance.

In my sophomore year I made an attempt—more of a cry for help—at killing myself. I ate an entire bottle of Midol. No doubt I would've taken something more potent than a bottle of period pain pills if I were actually serious. But, a cry for help it really was, because life had become painful for the teenage me. Friends were dropping like flies, mom and I fought all the time, and I was exhausted from working two jobs. My periods were out of control painful, landing me in the nurses' office each time they sporadically visited, and—most trying of all— there was Dad.

Dad was getting worse.

I desperately wanted escape. Mom and Dad found me on my bedroom floor, dizzy and weak from all the pills I'd downed. They dragged me into the bathroom and put me into a cold shower. When Dad said he'd pray for me, I screamed. When he actually began praying, but lecture-praying, I wished I'd actually succeeded in knocking myself off. There was no other escape.

Life was particularly excruciating when Dad took to proselytizing. My sweet-sixteen surprise party ended with the loss of a few terrified friends because of Dad's enthusiasm for Jesus. Terrified is a bit of stretch. Let's use confused instead. While the girls and I talked about the boys we liked, listened to good ole Lionel Richie, and played a silly word game, Dad entered the room, evangelizing with his tattered Bible.

It was awkward. Embarrassing. It caused three of the four girls to call their parents, forgoing the sleepover in an effort to get the hell away. I was jealous of their vanilla families with no Bible-bashing weird guy interrupting their lives. The way they left, with their near panic, you'd think my dad was trying to spread the Bubonic Plague rather than the Word of God.

Looking back as an adult now, I see how trivial it seems, but I lost those friends forever. Not only that, Dad's behavior changed something in me that night. It wasn't his fault, I knew that much.

I can't say that what changed in me that night was bad. I learned years later, that the experience taught me how to succeed. I realized that if I were going to get through my teen years with my sanity intact, I'd have to be patient. I realized that if I were going to be patient, successfully, I'd need to be persistent. I'd need to firmly move forward in life, but be patient with what life threw at me. I'd have to somehow triumph over all of this shit.

Persistence and Patience became my life motto. It was an inadvertent gift from my dad on the night of my sweet sixteenth birthday. ~~Thank you, Jesus.~~ Thanks Dad.

During the years of Dad's 'illness', came years of peculiar behavior. Bringing home a hooker still stands out as one of the most memorable. He'd pick me up on my walk home from school if he happened to be passing by. This day, I was almost home. I climbed into his beat up old baby blue Chevy pickup truck. Dad doubled back, pulled over, and waved in a prostitute.

I'd passed her before and thought she looked pretty rough. She wore a blue mini skirt, had red Peg Bundy hair that smelled of my grandmas old closet, and wore a ratty, funky smelling cheetah-print fur jacket. I supposed it was the aroma of weeks old sex. She had a white wife beater tank top on, no shoes and dirty fingernails that were chewed down to their nubs. A vivid memory. And there I was, nestled in the cab between she and my dad. Chummy. Even as a young kid, I knew what this woman was. I knew where Cheetah Woman came from—probably my old trailer park in Graham. By then, we'd moved from the trailer park into our much nicer, quaint home with an apple, pear and cherry tree with bushes of delicious raspberries in the back yard. Hookers in our town of Puyallup were common, but not really on our side of town.

Bringing home this woman on no planet should've been considered a good idea. My mom was going to flip her shit.

Luckily, though, mom wasn't home.

It was crystal clear that all Dad wanted was to give a hot meal to Cheetah Woman. I was oblivious to the fact that Dad really just wanted to help, distracted by her animalistic way of eating the leftovers—confused by the entire exchange. Did I mention she smelled? And she was silent. The lady never spoke. Literally never mumbled a word, she simply looked only at her lasagna. Maybe she was a mute? When she finished every delicious scrap on her plate, Cheetah Woman got up from the table, looked at us, and exited. No thank you (how rude), no request for money. Just a hot meal and gone. That was my dad, the kindest man alive.

Dad's Good Samaritan phase wasn't always just simply weird, sometimes it had more lasting consequences. Like the time he gave a homeless guy money. And by money, I mean my parents' entire savings account. Dad felt sorry for the guy, and thought a couple of bucks wouldn't do it. He wanted to help the man get started again. Jesus, or no Jesus, Dad was always generous. I hope you enjoyed the money I could've gotten braces with, homeless man. You needed it more than we did.

My dad used to stand on the roof of our house wearing his bathrobe and rubber boots in the pouring rain, drinking a warm cup of coffee with his face turned to the Heavens, letting the cold rain wash his face. He was probably chatting it up with the good ole Lord. Did I mention the Lord was making it rain?

Our helpful neighbor Virginia used to call and announce, "Your dad—he's doing that roof thing again."

To Dad, it was perfectly acceptable, normal behavior. He could see the whole neighborhood from up there. He was closer to God up there. It was peaceful place for him, away from the world and phone calls from our helpful neighbors, for one.

Dad believed for a short time that my mom was a 'biblical whore'. Honestly, Dad. What the fuck is a biblical whore, anyway? She sounds kind of fun, actually. What I cared about most, though, was that he wanted to exorcize our home of the demons inside it. It was a pretty scary, very rough time for a teenager. I was vulnerable, and my own flesh and blood thought our home was possessed by satanic entities. I knew it was just talk, that it was just the 'illness' speaking. He never made good on his promise to go all Father Karras on our demonic asses, either. Too bad, that would've made for an exciting chapter. Instead, he turned his attention to building a monster tree house out in the backyard for his kids—a more normal thing for a dad to do. We cut the pine tree's top clean off and perched the best damn tree fort/platform we'd ever dreamed of right smack on top of that poor, headless tree.

This is what our family dealt with on a daily basis, these swings between sanity and crazy, happy and sad—high and low. Just when Dad seemed not so 'Dad' anymore, he'd go and do something overly 'dad' like help my brothers and I build a tree fort.

Inevitably, sadly, Dad was admitted to a Mental Institution. Not sure how long it was, but in teenager time, it seemed to be years, because this girl needed her dad back. Life was happening too fast, and I was beginning to spiral out of control. I couldn't stop thinking about suicide, and these were the years when I was the most impressionable.

Our times with Dad were spent with that darn Bible around, and with him praying, I missed him. I missed him being physically close by. I missed the smell of his aftershave. Even in crazy years, Dad still shaved. That was our normalcy. I was so desperate; I even missed the putrid smell of his favorite canned soup—split pea—permeating the entire house.

"I need help with my homework, Dad."

"Dad, I need a hug."

"I made it to ensemble contest for choir, Dad. Can you come watch me sing? They only pick twelve girls of the seventy-five girl choir for it—aren't you proud, Dad?"

"Dad, I met this guy, and I like him, but he hits me sometimes, dad. Dad?"

But Dad wasn't there, not emotionally at least. It crushed my soul to wonder if I'd ever really truly have him back again.

I remember visiting him in the asylum—er mental ward—in the hospital. It was an unusual experience for a teenager to accompany one of her younger siblings to a mental hospital to visit their crazy dad.

Up until then, there was still no actual name for what was wrong with him. There was speculation, and words thrown around like 'depression', 'bipolar', 'manic-depression', 'chemically-imbalanced', 'psychotic', 'schizophrenic'.

And other than diagnosing him by looking through Encyclopedias and Psychology Books, Mom wasn't much help. She pretended all was normal in Jesus Dad land. Mom was a zombie on the hospital visit. Complete emotional shutdown. I don't blame her, it was simply my mom's way of coping.

The Mental Ward floor was like something from an intense psychological thriller. I saw bodies swaying to whatever sounds they were hearing in their heads. Vacant looks, unpleasant, erratic humming to no music, seemingly harried and scattered patients shuffling aimlessly while they drooled and moaned.

A large lady wearing a pink bathrobe and Santa slippers offered us some Easter Candy as soon as we stepped out of the elevator onto the eleventh floor—Dad's floor. What's that crap on her face? I wondered. Is that—yeah, that's definitely mustard.

"Ya want some of this heeeeeere candy, Little Girl?" she rasped, scaring me out of my wits as she licked her clearly sticky, chocolatey fingertips. At least...I think it was chocolate.

"Uh, no thanks," I said, as my youngest brother was reaching for it. "Tyson, no!" I shrieked.

"But, Jes—" I cut him off before he could finish his sentence.

"We have to go see my dad, now, thank you for the kind offer, Miss."

"You'll beeeeee back. They alllllllll come back!" Santa Slippers cackled as we speed walked towards my dad's room.

Who is 'they' and why do they always come back? I wondered as I choked back vomit pooling in the back of my throat.

I'm sure the candy wasn't poisoned, but it *was* Easter candy and this was September. After the encounter with the candy gatekeeper, almost the second I arrived, I wanted to leave...

I struggled to regain my composure. I told myself we were here for my dad, and I needed to be brave. After all, I reasoned, he'd be anxious to see us.

In the midst of all this, there was my dear old dad. He had on a new pair of glasses. It was the clearest memory I have of his room there. Dad hadn't worn glasses before, and now he had on a set of impressively round coke bottles. They made his eyes look bug-huge, watery, every eyelash around his eyes looked fake, painted on. *Is he wearing eye makeup?* I'd never seen such details in my dads' eyes on any day before that, or any day after. I should draw them. Had the illness affected his sight, as well?

He was lying in a bed, like he was physically sick, with his Bible. He always had the Bible. He probably needed to keep the Bible nearby just to fend off the spawn of Santa chocolate loving neighbor with it. He talked slow and drunkenly, like he was on drugs—he was on strong meds for sure.

We ended up staying for quite a while, sitting in a chair alongside Dad's bed. But it wasn't because he wouldn't let us leave. Most of that time I spent trying to attract his attention.

"Dad?"

"Dad? Tyson and Mom and I came to visit you."

"Dad? Why is your neighbor wearing Santa Slippers?

"Because it's cold, Jess-i-ca" he said.

That's a reasonable answer—okay he makes a good point.

Dad read that damn Bible the entire visit. We watched him intently, my younger brother and I. He didn't say more than the four words he used to acknowledge the lady in Santa slippers. I'm positive it was because he didn't know what to say to us.

As I kissed his forehead and we said our goodbyes after our mostly silent, invisible visit, I had a thought that helped me cope with the surreal situation. I decided that it was fine he didn't answer when I spoke, because this man wasn't even my dad. I wouldn't have known what to say to this stranger, anyway.

That Good Book began to stand for everything I hated. It stood for not having my dad around anymore and was responsible for his lack of interaction and engagement with his family. He buried his nose in the Bible, ignoring life and people around him.

He missed many of my teen years as they came and went. Instead, the stranger with the Bible was there like a ghost wearing dads' clothes and even eating his split-pea soup.

Every night, I fervently prayed to that picture of handsome Jesus that I was feeling more and more resentment towards. It was the same popular children's prayer with a few changes...

"Now I lay me down to sleep, I pray the Lord my soul to keep, and if I die before I wake, I pray my soul, the Lord to take. If the Lord shall take my soul, please take care of my mom, fix my dad, and take care of my brothers, my friends, and everyone I know. Amen."

And, every night, handsome Jesus ignored my prayers. I repeated that prayer for a solid ten years, until one night, I stopped. I gave up on Church, on religion, and on the thought that someday my lovely dad would be better—normal again.

I got rid of the picture of Handsome Jesus. I sold him at a garage sale—the same way he'd come into my life. The picture represented pain. It stood for cold hard judgment from other Churchgoers and it stood for undeserved misery for my family. This became the reason I gave up on having faith in this invisible God that had infected our lives.

I'd 'accepted Jesus Christ into my heart'. I'd attended Church and read the Bible during bible studies. I attended Youth Group and was *alive* for Christ. I went on mission trips, built Churches and led Bible studies. I was told he was testing me, our family.

I harbored hurt and confusion over those lost teenage years for more than twenty years.

But then, sitting in my Utah living room around a Christmas tree with my family, I finally broached the subject with my dad. Dad had been back to his 'normal' Dad self for many years by this point. We were all there, Mom, Dad, my brothers and their families, and my husband and kids. Dad had been diagnosed with Manic-Depression and Bi-polar. He was chemically imbalanced. But I still wasn't sure that the diagnosis explained the totally bizarre behavior that tore me apart when I was a teen.

"Dad, did they ever find out what triggered everything?" I asked, unsure if I was ready to hear the answer, if there was one.

Nothing could've prepared me for what he shared.

"Actually, Jess, yes. There was a man at work who was caught spiking the coffee pot with window cleaner and hits of acid."

Dad's doctors eventually worked out that it was very possible and highly likely that the poison in the cleaner, combined with the drug set off a chemical reaction in his brain that ultimately triggered his mental illness.

Kids, this is your brain...and this is your brain on window cleaner and acid.

My father explained the time as being similar to an overpowering acid trip. The poisons created hallucinations. He heard voices, saw things on the wall melting, spinning out of control. Before he knew it, his reality was forever changed.

What a fucking experience, and likely because of some careless asshole that fucked with my dad's brain.

My brothers perceive this time in our lives differently than I do, and Mom has her own series of experiences, Dad will definitely remember things differently (and he should consider writing his story, because it too will be different than mine). We each have our own perceptions of that time and have been impacted differently.

I worked two jobs at age sixteen for a reason.

It was all I could do to remove myself from the day-to-day home grind. It was my way of attempting to be invisible in an otherwise volatile existence.

My mom did her best, and I admire her for sticking it out, for better and for worse, in sickness and in health. Not many spouses can say that. Not many spouses can say they actually remained with their significant other through something as tumultuous as she did. Mom worked her ass off while Dad was in the hospital, and when his job put him on disability—not allowing him to come to work until a doctor cleared him—mom pulled overtime shifts at the local grocery store to pick up the slack. I'm proud to say that today, my mom and dad are better for it.

This experience with my dad was just another passing moment. We can remember how hard it was, the cabinets filled to the brim with pill bottles, and know that we are tough as nails as a family. We were patient, and persistent, we made it through—together.

And he wound up a bigger man after his illness. Dad became my hero, and I became a stronger woman during his illness.

I learned to be my own hero.

I didn't know how painful 'going viral' could be. It's a word every marketer is familiar with—and everyone wants a piece of.

When you've done something it seems everyone online knows about—is talking about, it's equal parts exciting and terrifying.

We were growing, and fast.

Mamabargains had already expanded beyond the garage. Our basement office was stuffed to the gills with product. We'd moved into and quickly outgrew a small warehouse space with an equally small Napoleon-complex landlord in the space of six months.

Mamabargains' success meant our business family had to increase in size as well.

Our team included a nanny for our two boys, a bookkeeper, an accountant, head developer, a customer service girl, a warehouse manager, three warehouse employees, my husband and I and a partridge in a pear tree—all dedicated to the success of Mamabargains.

Mamabargains was a twenty-four hour business, and I was there for practically every second of it. There's no clocking out when you're a business owner. You stay on the job, and most times, you do so without pay. You give one hundred twenty six hours a week, just to avoid working forty hours a week for someone else.

I don't recall opening my eyes each day, mostly because shutting them wasn't common practice. I'd sleep only for an hour or so at a time. Rolling over, I'd check my phone, responding to middle of the night customer service and vendor emails. Then I'd post to the Mamabargains Facebook page, sometimes putting out fires or tending to late night mama-drama on our multiple different social media networks. Tweets, Tumblr, Instagram, text, Facebook, Pinterest, Skype, or phone, I was constantly buried. I'd always wanted to be a social butterfly, instead, I'd become a slave to social media.

I was almost always the first to know when the site was down, or lagging. I'd be having conference calls with our developer and network/server administrators at 2am.

I'd personally deal with an angry customer whose order was late arriving, or a troll who just wanted to cause some trouble on social media. No job was too big, or too small for this CEO, and I learned that was a combination of both good *and* bad.

It didn't matter whether I was answering customer service calls, speaking to vendors, working in the warehouse, or cleaning toilets—I was a regular, daily fixture in the Mambargains world. I'd head home from the office between 6pm and 8pm, sometimes even later. Just because I physically left, didn't mean I wasn't still working. My phone always glued to my hand, my brain couldn't shut down.

The job of a CEO is to never truly tune out—that comes with the territory, regardless of the other parts of your life it kills.

There are only a certain number of hours in a day and I think I may have forgotten about Stanford somewhere between unclogging the office toilets, ass-whooping the social media trolls and taking those venture capitalist meetings. *Oh well,* I thought to myself a million times, *I'll remember to remember Stanford later. He'll understand.* Despite the workload, my kids seemed to be thriving. They had a nanny taking care of them, and she was awesome. I was confident all was mostly swell in family land as I plotted world domination.

We needed to find a sponsor of sorts. Mamabargains was making money, but I wanted to leverage the possibility of its potential long-term growth. Scalability, it's called.

If only I could find a great advertiser—someone who'd be interested in a strategic partnership.

When I think hard enough about things, I believe they can happen. This time was no exception.

I'd made multiple calls to a slew of huge companies—corporations I thought would align well with the Mamabargains brand. My goal was to get them excited about our feisty little business doing big things in its mere twelve months of operation.

Huggies Diapers, Luvs Diapers, Pampers, I considered each of them. They were the biggest household names out there that catered to families. *What about Johnson and Johnson? Colgate? Target? Kraft? Maybe Disney? Wouldn't all of these Fortune 500 companies be willing to partner with Mamabargains?* Anything is possible. So I approached every single one of them. I had nothing to lose, and only much to gain. I sent the multi-billion dollar corporations introductory emails.

Nothing happened. I'm not a great 'waiter.' Waiting has never gotten anyone anywhere. So I immediately sent follow-up emails, focusing on the persistence I'd learned as a kid. Then it happened.

And it happened while I was sitting there in my classy business attire of comfy pajamas, just fresh from sleep, eating a bowl of Grape Nuts (What? Hey, it isn't just seniors that need to stay *regular*.)

Through cereal and coffee, all things are possible. Dazed, and sort of confused after three hours or less of sleep, I perused my inbox. My customer service girl, Becca, had just arrived for her shift in my basement office when I saw it:

From: Emily @ Global Advertising Agency, NYC

Date: Wed, Aug 26th, 2009 at 1:30 PM

Subject: Opportunities with Luvs

To: jessica@mamabargains.com

Cc: Amanda @ GAA, Erica @ GAA

Hi Jessica,

I would like to set up a call to discuss future opportunities between Mamabargains and Luvs. We immediately fell in love with your site and have brainstormed a few ideas, and would like to hear yours as well. Below is an overview of the Luvs brand and our consumer.

Please let me know when you are available this week to discuss. I am available all day Friday (Eastern Standard Time).

Thanks,

Emily

My enthusiasm couldn't be contained as I stood up and began pacing. I pointed to the computer screen, motioning for Becca to give the email on my screen a read for herself.

Luvs Diapers is one of the largest diaper name brands on the planet. Be careful what you wish for—although my dream had just landed in my lap, I felt woefully underprepared for such high level negotiations. This was the big time, and I was feeling quite small.

"I'm so nervous, Becca! What do I say to a corporate conglomerate like Procter and Gamble?"

"You'll figure it out, Jess. You always figure it out. You can *do* this," said Becca.

The phone was sitting right in front of my face, ogling me, teasing me—begging me to use it. It taunted me. And I couldn't resist.

I picked it up and dialed the number.

Completely thrown for a loop, my voice trembled as I whispered my introduction, practicing my opening line while the line rang was more anxiety-inducing than reciting my own wedding vows.

Procter and Gamble? Holy shit!

I really hoped no one answered so I could just leave a mess—

"This is Emily, how can I help you?"

It was an awkward beginning to a conversation that I was unprepared for that rainy Utah morning, still sitting in in my pajamas. It marked the first conversation of many over several months of talks and negotiations with the global advertising agency representing Procter & Gamble—more specifically—Luvs Diapers. The negotiating I did on my own, and most times in my pajamas, and only *sometimes* munching away on cereal or toast—yes, I was getting very professional in the way I muted the phone as I chomped away on my Grape Nuts (those things are *loud!*). I'd sit in my basement on conference calls with upper executives from Procter and Gamble itself, and fend off complex questions they fired my way. Many of them I had absolutely no idea how to answer on the spot.

JESSICA SINGER | 97

"So, Jessica, please tell us what a partnership of this scale would cost?"

"Um..." NO, Jess. No um's or er's, that sounds wishy washy— unprofessional.

"How could Mamabargains help scale the social media following of the Luvs brand Facebook page from an under 10k fan base, to double or even triple that, organically?

"Er..." *Dammit, Jess. You don't sound confident at all. This is the big leagues!*

"Tell us what your ideas are on how we could best align our two brands in order to grow the Luvs Diapers brand."

"Hmmm..." *Okay, now you're just pissing me off. Buck the fuck up and be BIG.*

"We'd like to take a look at the Mamabargains P&L Statement. Can you please provide that along with its average rate of growth and financial projections for the upcoming year?"

"Well..." *'Well?' That's all ya got? Grrr. Give them something better, Jess!*

We were negotiating the particulars of a marketing partnership that would certainly catapult Mamabargains into the big time, but would our numbers be impressive enough to them?

They'd be looking at our financials, all of our stats and unique website hits, in order to determine the partnership likelihood.

After the um, er, hmmm, and well, my go-to 'I-don't-know-how-to-answer-your-question' kind of response was inevitably, "Let me get back to you once I run some numbers." I needed time to consider the implications of a small business strategically partnering with a huge corporation. There were so many variables, and this was such new territory for a company that twelve months ago didn't even exist.

Would Mamabargains become lost under the big name of Luvs, losing its brand identity—it's voice—in the process?

What would our loyal fans think?

Could teeny-tiny Mamabargains actually grow Luvs, the big-huge-behemoth brand?

I needed to consider what we were able to offer to them, and what they were able to offer in return. Most importantly, I needed to work out the cost of the entire partnership.

This is just sales, Jess, simple sales. Don't make it more difficult than it needs to be. Just approach it like you would with the vendors of Mamabargains. What are the benefits to the vendor? Approach it from that angle. What are the positives for Luvs?

In a nutshell, they wanted a bigger social media following, and Mamabargains' fan base was ten times theirs at that point. In exchange, they'd pay us. They'd require their logo on our home page. We'd be required to offer Luvs diapers as a feature on Mamabargains, and we'd have to give their Facebook followers a preview of one Mamabargains feature per week—the exact item, time and date it would feature.

Hold the phone—this was unheard of at Mamabargains— it was literally priceless, top secret information. Our fans would do anything for even the smallest 'hint' about one of our deals per week. The only way they'd get it would be to follow the Luvs' page. We had full confidence that the brilliant strategy would work, but it was still a huge gamble for us, and I had a lot of questions of my own.

This would basically alter the entire way Mamabargains functioned. I wasn't so sure our fans would approve, but the financial reward meant we could grow, thus bringing our customers even more deals.

Since Mamabargains only posted a deal of the moment (the only deal site of it's kind as others only offered deal of the day or deal of the week), you never knew when one deal would switch, and you definitely never knew what it was going to switch to.

It paid to check in with Mamabargains all day long. To get in on the best deals, like the baby carriers, cloth diapers or even the strollers, you had to keep coming back. Fans became 'one with the refresh button' on their keyboards. They quickly became addicted to the constantly rotating deals. In fact, our slogan was, 'Common Sense caution: Our site is addictive—Are YOU Hooked Yet?'

We'd cleverly built something that Luvs wanted for themselves. We created the 'get it before its gone frenzy' with our deal of the moment offerings. Their primary objective? Luvs desperately wanted the engagement of their own fans, and they also wanted our fans and our shoppers to become theirs as well. .

Could we clone our social media savvy, migrating it into positive growth for Luvs, or would this undo all we'd worked so hard for? If fans/shoppers were able to get a preview of what one offering per week was just by following Luvs, I wondered if our sales would be negatively or positively impacted?

What would make those fans still want to check in to see what deals are popping up if they were already getting the Luvs preview? Would the buyer frenzy disappear? Or what if our fans hated Luvs, or worse, what if they hated what Procter and Gamble stood for? Would we end up *losing* fans in the processing of trying to *grow?*

Jesus, there were so many variables.

I figured if I just came up with a number to offer as the value of the partnership that wasn't too low or way too high, that they'd bite. Or would they? It was all going to come down to this total. We could accomplish everything they wanted and needed of Mamabargains—I knew our team was more than capable. It seemed to be a more than fair trade off.

Certainly they'd question, though, how I came up with the number I crunched.

Is this one of those times I could just toss a figure out there and wing it?

I decided to go with the latter. Winging it had always worked in my favor before.

My heart raced as I prepared to drop the magic amount in their laps. I thought I might throw up, right then and there, because the six digits seemed higher than I felt completely confident with, but Luvs was huge. Procter and Gamble, even larger. They could handle it. This partnership would be worth more than I'd ever dreamed of making in an entire year, and almost two years worth of my husband's yearly salary.

I held my breath, wishing I had some magic anxiety pill to pop.

Maybe they'd hang up, or laugh, or...

They. Didn't. Bat. An. Eye.

Not only didn't the executives question the number, they didn't seem to care. I wondered whether I should've added a couple more greedy zeroes onto the end of my quote. I've never admitted this out loud. But it's true.

I drafted the contract myself, letting our attorney give it a good 'red-lining'.

After multiple iterations of contract revisions and negotiations that had taken up the better part of an entire year, Luvs finally signed the contract. The partnership we worked industriously through developing finally went live, June 2010. This was the game-changer I'd been dreaming of, the moment Mamabargains would lift-off into the big time. Not only that, signing with Proctor & Gamble would be our let up on Babysteals. I'd definitely buy lunch with a company credit card next time I met with my perfectly pretty competitor across town.

All in all, to Luvs, this was pocket change. To us, it meant new product, new employees, and it meant growth. Plus, we would have the diaper feature. It meant we could move our office from the basement of our tiny home into a larger warehouse space with an office.

It was a life-changing deal for Mamabargains.

Maybe we'd even have enough to start really paying ourselves, or at the very least, move out of our dumpy little house on a busy street where the kids couldn't even play out front because of the cars speeding by.

I was careful, though. I didn't want to be a statistic—one of those businesses that popped the corks on their champagne prematurely.

So we worked hard re-investing into our business. We turned vital growth dollars into a new six thousand square foot warehouse and office space. We'd come so far since the days when we only had $3600 in our savings account. We were helping local and national economic growth, albeit on a small scale. We were making it happen.

The Luvs deal meant a life within an unreal reality, reminiscent of an old Twilight Zone episode.

Fast-forward six months when all was going great—until going great became a stranger.

We decided to offer each box of diapers (which retailed for over $35) for just $11. We didn't want a huge profit on the diapers, we just wanted families to have a sweet deal. I can't describe how excited our entire staff was to offer those hugely discounted diapers to our fans—a big thank you to them for sticking with us. If you want to get a taste of the time capsuled action, Google 'Mamabargains Luvs Diapers.'

Luvs posted this to their Facebook page to get the ball rolling:

Here's a www.mamabargains.com sneak peak that you don't want to miss. Tomorrow Wednesday August 4th at 1:30 pm EST they will be featuring our very own Luvs diapers! These diapers will be sold by the box (each box will contain 4 jumbo packs) and will come in sizes 2, 3, 4, and 5. The limit will be 3 boxes per household... per size. Oh yeah, and one more thing...the average retail price of these boxes is $35.96, BUT they will be offered for $11.00 which will be 69% off of retail!

It would mark the very first time ever that a box of well-known brand-name disposable diapers would be that heavily discounted *anywhere*.

It was a hair-raising partnership because Mamabargains was contractually obligated to do so many things. Not only that, we'd expanded and brought on more staff.

After the teaser was posted, the Internet went mad. As in crazy. As in *viral*.

Hundreds of thousands of customers had heard about the diaper offering. Not only that, but now they knew exactly what day, what time and price point they'd be offered. It seemed smart to let Luvs give the Facebook fans a preview of Luvs diapers, right?

Wrong. We were so very wrong.

The moment the diapers went live on the site, more than one hundred thousand people tried to jump on the Mamabargains site at the same precise moment, and our servers simply couldn't handle the traffic. Even though we'd spent several weeks amping up on server space in anticipation of the big feature, no amount of staff or server preparation equipped us for what lay ahead. It was the very first time the Mamabargains site had *ever* crashed.

First time, and worst possible timing.

There was no way we could've known exactly how big this deal was going to be or forecast the deluge of new fans anxious to score a piece of history. Shit and piss absorbers. Who'd have thought?

Coincidentally, the Singers were on a rare, brief, had already been planned for months family vacation. Our burned out family needed this away time.

Luvs had made the decision *exactly* when they wanted us to feature the diapers and they let us know about a month prior what that date would be. I'll be damned if they didn't decide to have that huge feature go live right smack in the middle of our weekend getaway.

Where was it we had chosen to go that just so happened to fall on the occasion of the biggest launch in Mamabargains' life?

We were staying in a *cabin* in the *middle of nowhere* in Yellowstone National Park. A paradise. And a communications vortex. There was no phone signal, absolutely no Wi-Fi, and we'd left the carrier pigeons at home when the hemorrhaging began.

Our poor staff was mostly rolling solo while we raced to the nearest corner market to speak with our development team about how to resolve the nightmare. The site had completely crashed, the fallout caused complete and utter chaos.

We were complete and utter chaos.

With our kids by our sides, we dealt with the unfolding situation, right between the baked beans and cereal aisles. Pacing back and forth, our kids following behind us begging for a bag of marshmallows and graham crackers, we were met with strange glances from strangers. Stanford and I listened on the same phone, sharing a set of headphones, one bud in his ear, the other in mine. We must've looked like idiots and sounded like maniacs. We yelled—a lot. Our development team should've been prepared for this. The whole store knew that whatever it was we were dealing with, they were relieved to not be on the receiving end of this train wreck.

Our employees were flipping out, our customers were having mommy temper tantrums and our gargantuan corporate client—they were *completely* irate.

Customers were angry that they didn't score the deal. They were busy posting everywhere about how awful Mamabargains was for 'teasing' them with such a great deal, only to have the site take a shit while they tried to get the poop pants deal to load. The fucking irony.

Luvs didn't know how to handle the angry customers. They didn't realize that this notoriety, well, it was actually *helping* them grow more than they could've imagined. News travels fast in the online parenting world. Because of the site collapse, people were hearing about this amazing deal on diapers that hadn't even heard of Mamabargains, and had no idea of the Luvs diapers offering. It actually raised awareness for both companies.

Our employees were mystified over how to handle the hot mess. They were all busy deleting offensive comments posted on our social media pages about how horrible we were for 'letting' our site crash. Every parenting forum online was abuzz about the Luvs deal, and there were many that were bad mouthing Mamabargains for not having enough diapers to go around. As if we'd deliberately allowed our site to crash while they were trying to score their precious diapers.

No one realized, except those internal to the issue, just how traumatizing this experience was to our hard working employees, and to the Singers—stranded far from civilization up in the mountains.

Regardless of the drama that unfolded when our site was down for two whole days with *no revenue coming* in, it went down for the *right* reason. Thousands and thousands of new customers, desperate to be part of this huge promotion had made Luvs an even bigger name. And Mamabargains became a bigger name that day, too. Just Google 'Mamabargains Luvs Crash 2010'. Read for yourself.

After the launch of the partnership and just before the crash, we'd moved into a new warehouse space, hired more customer service employees, part time warehouse staff, a marketing professional, a PR firm, and a new development company to handle the sheer size that Mamabargains had so quickly grown to. The growth didn't have an end in sight. We did our best to prepare for all of it. Unfortunately you can't prepare yourself for the unknown. These new developers and network server administrators were there for us when the site overloaded with traffic. It took a few days, but thankfully they'd gotten us back on track.

But for how long? And at what cost?

You know what they say about success attracting success...

Mamabargains won a Stevie Award in 2010 for being the fastest growing company in the entire US of A. Think of what an Emmy looks like—Stevie is an Emmy, but for business professionals. The fifteen inch tall gold guy weighed almost twenty pounds. I still bittersweetly bring him out now and again to remind myself of our achievements. We also took fourth place in Startup Nations fan based, customer vote generated business competition—we were honored as the fourth coolest startup business in America. Pretty damn cool.

And the awards kept coming. Utah Business magazine recognized me as a prestigious '40 under 40' award recipient. Forty business owners under age forty— success stories to watch in the State of Utah.

I had my first television interview (it went well, except that unrelenting wedgie of mine).

I co-hosted a radio show (it went well, except filter-free Jessica shouldn't have used the word 'fuck' *on air*.)

We appeared on our first television talk show (it went well, except that little piece of black pepper I had in my teeth the entire time. How come they didn't tell me?)

Senator Bob Bennett of Utah asked me to speak at his rural business conference as a breakout session speaker. It went better than expected, going over its scheduled time by twenty minutes. The room was stuffed to the gills with men and women who wanted to be entrepreneurs. It was a pride filled moment as I answered all of their questions.

It seemed like all the hard work was paying off because CEO Jessica Singer suddenly had a lot of friends.

A day in the life at Mamabargains would make an awesome reality show, I often thought to myself. All of it was just non-stop adventure.

What they don't tell you is that you can also be blinded by the same success that lit you up. There were dark clouds gathering.

Stanford and I met for sushi once a week. That was the extent of our relationship. Bonding over tuna and sake. We talked about business and the kids, not *us*. We were lucky to make one home cooked meal a week. Most nights we came home from Mamabargains as late as 8pm, grabbing takeout on the way home. We were seeing each other mostly at Mamabargains. Good thing our nanny was there, doing the job we should've been doing.

I didn't know it then, but the lucrative partnership with Proctor and Gamble marked the beginning of trouble for Mamabargains.

Our viral world was unraveling.

Teens need support, and I wasn't getting any.

Dad was in a mental institution.

Mom was slowly slipping into what I can only guess was a major depression of her own after watching his meltdown.

My youngest brother was too young to care.

My other brother—there are not many words for him in general.

Kevin drove an ugly, bright lime green AMC Gremlin. And I fell prey to his troll-like advances.

I'd met Kevin before poet-drug-dealer Jake, and I'd also met him in English class. In tenth grade, English was my favorite of all subjects in school—probably should've learned sooner that it would've been best to just stick to Shakespeare and avoid fraternizing.

There was a beautifully, drawn to perfection dolphin waiting for me on my desk in English class. It had the words, 'Hello, Gorgeous!' written above it. Who would draw such a glorious thing? The '*gorgeous*' couldn't possibly mean me, could it?

I wrote a note back to the dolphin artist:

"Who are you? The dolphin is beautiful"

The next day, I received a response, which only deepened the mystery.

"Thanks, I think *you* are beautiful."

How could the dolphin drawer know such a thing?

Wait a minute! How the hell did that note stay on the desk through all the periods of the day without a single person erasing it?

Because it had to be the person who sat there during the period right before me—that's how. The 'note writing' went on for a week before I found time to stalk the hallway. Spying through the door window, I solved the mystery of my Romeo dolphin drawer.

There he was—a tall, lanky guy. Good-looking, but not exactly handsome. More—turtle-like.

The next five months with Kevin the dolphin-drawing turtle were blissfully romantic. We held hands. We kissed chastely. Kevin courted me like a gentleman should. No boyfriend had ever called me "beautiful" before Kevin.

Kevin would pick me up in the neon monster, bring me to school and drive me home afterwards. He'd hang out with me during the break between my job at the local pizza restaurant and my shift at the movie theater. He'd bring me flowers, and he gave me a gold cross necklace. I didn't much like gold, but I wore this beautiful necklace with pride for the love of Kevin and of God that it represented. And also because it must have cost him a small fortune.

In our fifth month of dating, Kevin and I laid in his bed. I wasn't allowed to be in a boy's bedroom with the door shut, but his parents weren't home this particular afternoon. We just said to hell with it, because I trusted him. Why wouldn't I, after the romantic months we'd spent together?

We kissed—a forgettable kiss during an unforgettable moment.

I was a virgin. (The relationship with Jake came months after this one)

I was wearing my homely jeans and a baggy sweatshirt with Goofy on it.

An episode of Beavis and Butthead was on in the background. The clock read 4:00 exactly. Kevin had his hands down my pants and I was mostly okay with that.

Maybe I led him on—because when I asked him to stop...

When I felt uncomfortable enough to tell him to remove his hands...

Kevin didn't.

Instead, he mashed four fingers directly inside me.

This was more than just uncomfortable—I'd never experienced such pain. Up until then, I'd drawn the line at dry humping and kissing, and one-fingered fun. A fully clothed, good groping session kept me satisfied.

Groping, this was not.

Unfortunately, Kevin wasn't finished. He threw the blankets off and crawled on top of me. The moment is chilling to relive.

He smelled of old man's cologne. The smell wafted into his bedroom, moments after we arrived at his house that afternoon. It was disgusting. I was distracted with the thought that he put that smelly shit on for me—his attempt at seduction.

With him now on top of me, I tried an unsure, "Please stop, Kevin."

But he didn't.

I then tried a slightly more stern, "Stop."

That didn't work either.

Next, with everything I had to give, "STOP! STOP RIGHT NOW! I AM NOT READY! STOP!"

You want to know what Kevin's response to my cries was?

"Shut up while I fuck the virgin out of you, you little whore."

Where was my sweet Kevin and who was this monster? Did someone pour water on him?

He painfully, repeatedly lunged. I lost count of how many times I asked, begged, cried, *screamed* for him to *STOP*. He just kept going. He slammed into my bleeding vagina while he drooled down onto me. The saliva was repulsive. His halitosis breath stunk the way my grandpa's did after a day in his dentures. The spit dripped onto the chest of my sweatshirt as he pounded away, careful not to look straight into my pleading eyes.

Kevin's eyes remained mostly closed. I hope he saw some guilt in that darkness of his because they certainly didn't shutter out my cries for him to stop.

He restrained my arms down by my sides, and because he'd pulled my slim jeans down to only just above my knees, they constricted my legs like handcuffs. My hips ached in agony with the worst of the pain instantly shooting down my legs and up my back with each one of his pelvic slams. I felt like my hip bones were going to break from the pressure of his heavy body thrusting on top of me. It was a claustrophobic nightmare, leaving my body convulsing.

I didn't realize I was sobbing. I didn't feel the tears running down my cheeks until Kevin screamed at me, "SHUT THE FUCK UP, YOU BABY! GO CLEAN UP AND THROW THIS AWAY. MAKE SURE YOU HIDE IT."

To add to the humiliation, he demanded I dispose of the dirty condom.

He hadn't put it on in front of me, but when he initially pulled his pants down I'd noticed the thing was already there. His premeditation warned me what was about to happen, but before I could stop it, his body weight was already on top of me. Too late.

As Kevin pulled his pants up, I noticed a tattoo on his ankle. Desperate to change the subject, to distract my mind, I asked him through tears what the small, clearly homemade tattoo represented. He told me that it symbolized his favorite punk band, 'The Meatmen.' Oddly fitting.

So much for the distraction. This person represented pure evil.

I pulled my pants up over my swollen, bleeding vagina and looked down at his bed. Based on the pain I'd just endured, I expected the bed would look like a massacre had just taken place. While it felt like he was stabbing me with a knife, only a small amount of blood remained on the sheets. His weapon of choice, a penis, had done more damage than a knife could have.

It felt like hours had passed. But the same episode of Beavis and Butthead played on the TV, and the time on the clock read 4:06pm.

Kevin knew from the moment we got to his room that he was going to have sex with me, whether I wanted it or not. Maybe he'd planned his heinous act for longer than the afternoon. He knew I wasn't ready, because I'd told him just that through tears. I'd begged him to stop, but he just didn't care. No matter what my reaction, Kevin was going to take what he wanted that day.

The agony had turned the six minutes of rape time into what felt like hours of torture.

Walking was painful. My hips wanted to give out on me. My knees were weak, and my entire body was racked by a wave of nausea. I couldn't get out of his room fast enough.

I had an escape plan, but knew better than to attempt it. His house was out in the boonies. I'd be fleeing from him for a long time along deserted, rural roads. I imagined him running me down with his evil Gremlin. I'd be dead by the end of the day at this rate. I had no option but to do as I was told.

I went to the bathroom and looked at myself in the mirror. This was when I realized exactly how hard I must've been crying. My eyes were a shade of red that I didn't recognize. My face was flush. My hair disheveled. The only item of clothing that he hadn't touched was my sweatshirt, except with his drool. I found myself feeling grateful that at least he didn't grope my little A-cup mosquito bites. I swore to myself in the mirror that he'd never get the chance to touch me again.

I tucked the disgusting condom in the garbage can, dutifully hiding it under several layers of toilet paper. Around my neck hung the cross necklace he'd sweetly given me after I shared with him the fact that my dad was 'sick'—that we still didn't know exactly what was wrong with him.

Where is my God? I need Him.

Just as I was about to take the necklace off, I heard the front door shut.

Kevin's mom was home, and he barged into the bathroom, nervous, whisper yelling, *"You better not say a fucking word to my mom, or to anyone else."*

Overwhelmed with exhaustion, pain and now the threat of violence, I plastered on my smile, pretending that everything was swell in Jessica-land.

His mother greeted me with a happy, yet puzzled look on her face. "Is that my necklace?" And then more firmly, "Jessica, did you *steal* my necklace? It's been missing for weeks!"

No, I didn't steal your necklace. Kevin gave it to me. Your rapist son, the virginity thief, who just violated me in his bedroom while Beavis and Butthead heehawed in the background—he stole it. I hope he rots in whatever you consider hell.

I wished I'd said what I was thinking, but in the sick reality I was in, I actually said, "No, I didn't steal it, Kevin just let me borrow it. He's always so sweet." I'd complimented a rapist, and in front of his mom, who was now smiling ear-to-ear. She was beaming with pride at how 'sweet' her son was to me.

You're welcome, you asshole.

In the lime green car, on the drive back to the safety of my home, only silence. The rapist didn't say a word. His terrified victim kept her lips sealed. Both of them.

I found it hard to breathe—scared he was going to take me somewhere and rape me again. I wanted to die. I wanted to jump from the moving vehicle and be run over by the cars in its wake. I wanted to wash away all that was left inside me, taken from my soul.

We arrived at my house, just as my mom was getting home from her grocery store shift. The rapist walked around to the passenger side and opened my door, extending his hand to assist me out of his vehicle. He fabricated gentlemanly ways to his victim's unassuming mom, who was watching the darling scene unfold in front of her eyes.

I didn't smile at him. Instead, I unchained the necklace from my neck, which had now come to represent being shackled to Kevin the rapist, and dropped it onto the passenger seat. I couldn't bring myself to place it into his open, abusive hand. I refused to touch him.

I wonder if Mom realized that something was wrong? If she did, she didn't let on. I grabbed my backpack and walked into the house. I didn't look back at the rapist. I didn't offer a goodbye. I knew I was walking away from that horrible human being forever.

We never spoke again. What he left me with was a wound that was entirely too large for me to heal on my own.

My totally naïve best friend, Marie, a complete Bible thumper, noticed that I seemed off, but didn't question it. I wasn't sure how or if I'd ever tell her. She knew that Kevin and I had broken up—I wasn't sure she needed to know more. Marie had never even had a phone call with a boy, because her family was incredibly strict. How would I ever explain to her that my boyfriend had raped me without seriously traumatizing her?

A few weeks after the rape, I realized I couldn't keep the secret any longer. I needed support. I hadn't previously told anyone because I couldn't find the words. I grappled with the thought that it was my fault. That he was my boyfriend, and because of that, maybe it was my fault. But slowly I'd have to learn to leave the victimization of my innocence behind.

Marie deserved to know the truth. She was my best friend, and I needed her.

"The reason why Kevin and I are not together anymore is because I'm no longer a virgin. I ended it because of that." The simple explanation would hopefully be enough for my devoutly sinless friend.

"Oh."

That was it. The conversation my best friend and I had about my boyfriend, about our breakup, about my *rape*.

I was *devastated.*

I thought that despite being sheltered, she was smart enough to figure out what my words had meant. I actually hoped she'd be curious enough to start a conversation about it. I needed her to want to know what the circumstances were. But she didn't ask, ever. So I didn't tell. I didn't want to say the word 'rape' out loud. I couldn't.

Soon after, Marie began dodging me. She avoided meeting up after class like we'd done every day since we met in 6th grade. She stopped returning my calls. We didn't ride together to Church youth group anymore. Something was off.

After youth group one week, Marie finally spoke to me for the first time in weeks.

"I'm going to go on the next Church mission trip to Alaska this summer. I don't want you to come".

We'd gone to Mexico the year before to help build a church. A year prior to that, we'd gone to Canada to do the same.

It was our 'thing', these mission trips over the summers.

The Canada mission trip had brought pain for me, but closeness for Marie and I. A family that I had regularly babysat for lost their twenty-month-old daughter to what we later found out was S.I.D.S. We were on the mission trip when I received the call about her death. I was grateful for Marie and her mom's support while I was so far from home. I was unable to attend the funeral for baby Lindsay because we were hard at work helping to rebuild this Church. This was our mission, our gift to God. I was confused at how a baby could die, and dejected by her loss. I was curious and angry with God for taking such an innocent soul from the world, and Marie consoled me.

I'd begun to lose faith in these days.

The loss of my dads mental stability, my virginity, baby Lindsay, and now Marie?

"Okay, I guess if you don't want me to go, then I won't," I said.

Still wondering what I'd done to make her so angry, I spent the summer after tenth grade agonizing over how I'd managed to alienate my best friend. She was slipping away from me.

What *had* I *done*?

Marie's return from Alaska only a few months later answered all of my questions, plus some.

It happened right before eleventh grade was to begin and I'd missed her all summer long. I was lonely without my best friend. She was my only confidant, not my only friend, but the one I shared *almost* everything with.

"Hey, Jessica, it's Marie. I'm back from Alaska. Can my mom drop me off at your house for a little bit?" she asked.

It was unusual, because her mom rarely allowed her to come to my house. We typically had to go to her house to hang out. Maybe because the dog posters plastered all over the walls to her bedroom were more 'pure' than my song lyrics, movie posters and dark poetry adorning my walls. Joey McIntyre and the New Kids on The Block didn't help my case, either. Because they played soft pop rock, and our Nazarene Church taught us all about how demonic rock music was. Darn that satanic Joey poster hanging above my bed!

Marie sat down on my bed, immediately blurting out, "*God* told me that I'm not *allowed* to be your friend anymore".

Wow. She sure didn't waste any time.

Evidently I was a bad influence, but by *God*, I think what she actually meant was her *overbearing mother*. I knew she was the real source.

Our five-year-long friendship was over, just like that, with her lie, and my own lie by omission. Marie went on to say that our lives were going in different directions, "I need to focus on God, not you and your *unimportant* issues".

There you go again, God, stealing my loved ones. What a kind, loving, generous God you are!

Before Marie left our twenty-minute visit, she had one more little parting gift for me.

"*My* mom is going to tell *your* mom that you had *s-e-x* (she actually whisper-spelled the word *sex*, as if she was trying to make sure God didn't hear). If you don't want my mom to tell your mom, you better tell her first." And with that, she was gone.

Her mom was still there, sitting in her car in our driveway, waiting for Marie to dump me.

Moments after she left, my mom found me in my room, inconsolable. I explained to her what happened.

"She broke up with me, Mom," I said through the tears I'd become overly accustomed to shedding.

I knew that I needed to heed Marie's warning. She wouldn't lie about what her mom was planning. I'd planned to never tell my parents. I was only sixteen. I lost my virginity at sixteen. Lost? My virginity was *stolen* at sixteen.

Starting from the beginning, I explained everything to my mom. I spared the gross details of what happened to me those many months ago with Kevin. I gave her the reasons why I felt Marie was 'breaking up' with me. I felt so dirty.

My mother cried with me. It was a moment of closeness that I'll always treasure because it gave us a long lost connection that we hadn't felt in quite some time.

The silver lining was that my dad had just arrived home from being in the mental institution. He wasn't the same old dad—the still-full, unopened beer cans in the refrigerator were evidence enough, but I was grateful for his fatherly presence.

Mom told him everything, leaving him understandably distraught—angry. I realized if he'd had gun at that moment, he might still be incarcerated today for the crime I knew he wanted to commit.

Meanwhile, as my mom and I sat on the floor crying, my Church Youth Group Pastor was meeting with Marie's parents. They were apparently 'so distressed' that their daughter was the best friend of a *whore* that they needed to discuss it with the Church. The Pastor, being one of God's friends, contacted my mom and dad. He wanted to have a group meeting to discuss myself and Marie as well as 'other issues' that they needed to 'get out into the open'.

"Hello there, this is Jeff, the Youth Pastor. I'd like to meet with you, along with Marie and her parents, but without Jessica present. Could you come to my office this evening?" the caring counselor asked my mom.

"Um, of course, we will be there in an hour," she responded.

My parents felt the friction on the other end of the phone. They sensed the urgency of the situation and obliged. They believed that after a careful discussion, everything would return to normal and I'd have my best friend back. I should've smelled a rat when Jeff didn't invite me to the powwow. I'm so glad they had a *qualified* person to persecute me for being raped, though. That must've made them feel like real winners.

I suppose I'd have to stay home, sewing a scarlet letter on all of my clothing. The shame.

According to my mom, within the first ten minutes of the ~~conversation~~ inquisition, Marie's mom blurted out, "Did you know that Jessica is having *s-e-x* (there we go with the whisper-spelling, again) with her boyfriend?"

Marie's dad evenly, calmly sat in the corner of the room, arms crossed, no words coming out of his mouth.

My mom was livid. She stayed calm, as she explained, "We are *aware* that Jessica is no longer a virgin. There are circumstances that you are *not* aware of and that Jessica doesn't want *you* to be aware of because it's a very personal and *private* matter."

"Your daughter is promiscuous! I don't want Jessica ever coming over again, and she is not to speak to Marie in future. I'll be taking Marie out of all of the classes she has with Jessica".

"I don't think it's a good idea for Jessica to return to our Youth Group," Jeff said point-blankly.

"Why don't you look in the mirror, judge yourselves—or better yet, why don't you judge the fucker that *raped* our daughter!" My mom shouted their direction, grasping for breath as the angry words escaped her mouth.

Mom and Dad stood up, with only Mom's last sentence being exchanged—she got her last, powerful words in.

"Some fucking Christians *you all* are!" She added, a full-blown asthma attack bearing down on her, stealing her breaths.

I don't think mom and dad wanted to give them another minute of their time. They had a daughter back at home they needed to be there for. And what happened to her was *none of the Godly folks' goddamned business*. Plus, mom needed her inhaler.

Do not judge, and you will not be judged. Do not condemn, and you will not be condemned. Forgive, and you will be forgiven. Even I had learned that Bible verse in Youth Group. Apparently Jeff the Pastor, and Marie's parents decided *their* rules were better than God's. Judgy bastards.

The next day at school, Marie was no longer in any of my classes. Her parents yanked her forcedly from my life in the blink of an eye, making good on the threats they'd given my parents. We'd pass each other between classes like strangers.

Like father, like daughter, I suppose. Now I had my own record of being expelled from God's house.

Jessica, the sinner, the whore.

How dare I let myself get *raped*? How. *Dare*. I.

This would prove to be the more catastrophic of the two experiences that traumatic year. I was getting stronger every day, and could even handle the rape. What I didn't think I could cope with was being heart-raped by my best friend, and then again by her asshat parents. God didn't do me any favors, either.

Look around you, Jess. There is life everywhere, it's inside your heart.

Surround yourself with people who see—feel—this in you.

With the technical support of our new development team Mamabargains soared.

We'd hired them during the Procter and Gamble/Luvs diaper crash, and alongside Gregg, our head of IT, they'd provided all the tech support we required. Stanford came onto Mamabargains part time as the CFO—a daily fixture, he'd help lead the ever-growing task list.

There comes a time in many businesses when you outgrow what you never thought you'd outgrow. That time had come as Mamabargains continually surpassed each goal we'd set.

That's the fun stuff to write about, the greatness. The most challenging chapters to pen—to relive, are *these* ones. The nitty gritty details of what crushed us.

As a company grows, so does its overhead.

We'd finally begun paying ourselves. I was getting compensation for the 120+ hours I was putting in every week. When I did the math, I was making $2 less than that of my sales girl, Becca. Mamabargains was my baby, and we make sacrifices for our babies.

A year passed, and we continued along our path of exceptional growth.

Utah IT increased their fee. Bastards! Our monthly rate for the first year with them was going to exponentially rise at the end of the year. After trying to renegotiate the contract, to no avail, it was time to replace them. They had dollar signs in their eyes where Mamabargains was concerned. They could see our potential. They wanted to line their pockets with Mamabargains' cash flow.

The language of code within a website is it's heart—the foundation on which the site is built. There's a major learning curve in becoming a skilled developer on a custom website. Since Mamabargains was 100% custom, that meant we didn't have a pre-existing or plug-in shopping cart. We didn't have a ready-made website, it was developed by us from the ground up.

Gregg and I brainstormed needed improvements daily. He'd always confidently say, "Nothing's impossible, Jessica". Then he'd work hard to make it happen. Our hunt was on for another local IT company with deep knowledge, entrepreneurial spirit, and of course, better rates.

They'd have to offer 24/7 support since our website never closed. We required around the clock availability, because website crashes happen—we'd seen it with the Luvs Diapers' crash (and we all know how fun *that* debacle was!). Server management and monitoring to maintain our customer database (emails, phone numbers, addresses, order details, etc.) and the coding Gregg had created would be crucial. Network security was also essential (like a locked mailbox where mail is safely stored, only accessible with a key). The most important necessity, though, was firewall protection on every server (picture several homes with all of its windows and doors open—we needed locks on those doors and windows, and someone to monitor to make sure no one broke in).

Finding a company to look after all these essentials was proving difficult.

James (though I'd love to refer to him as Dick Wad), one of the lead consultants working for Utah IT, privately approached us. James had signed a non-compete clause with them, but said he had his own company that could look after Mamabargains' digital needs. He'd worked with us for a year already, just indirectly. He *knew* our code. He knew *Mamabargains*.

We'd found our solution! What a relief! And he sold it well:

"My company will provide everything you had at Utah IT and more. Personal service—you'll be working *directly* with me, rather than working with me *through* Utah IT. Lower rates—we will be less than half of what they were charging before their price hike."

"My biggest concern is database and server security along with 24/7 availability. It's a deal-breaker without it. Is that possible?"

"We have offices in Texas, Utah, Washington, London and India," James assured, an arrogant undertone present in his voice. "You'll have around the clock coverage."

He's probably working out of his basement and eating cereal in his pajamas right now. Takes one to know one, Jess. You should trust people, more, woman!

"Sounds like a win-win since you won't have a learning curve. You've already indirectly worked with Mamabargains. Let me discuss with Stanford."

What an asshole he was—borderline pompous. Just because he sounds like an ass, doesn't mean he's inexperienced, though. I've known many successful shitheads.

"This conversation is confidential. Don't email me through your Mamabargains email. Create a temporary one so Utah IT can't see us communicating."

I suppose it was a fair enough request for confidentiality. Utah IT *did* manage our email servers, so they *could* technically see all our emails if they wanted to.

With weeks left on our Utah IT contract, Stanford and I decided to take ~~Dick Wad~~ James up on his offer. It was financially feasible—plus, we were out of options.

Blinded to the many warning signs, mistake number one was made.

He called his company 'Your Utah IT Services' and from this point forward, we'll refer to them as YUITS (although I'd prefer to refer to them as Asshateus Maximus, Inc.).

James appointed a project manager, Damon (the demon), to be the direct line of communication between Mamabargains and YUITS. He'd handle all help requests.

"What previous experience does Damon have in technical project management and Ecommerce?" I asked James.

"He's been with us a long time. He has an extensive background. You'll sign the first six month contract with Damon rather than YUITS, so I'm in the clear in case Utah IT discovers I'm working for you."

Sly bastard.

"That seems odd, but I get it," I said, out of options and needing to move forward.

It was clear their misguided moral compass was going to eat away at me. It didn't help either that my gut was screaming, *run for the hills!* Something was off. They were trying to get around the non-compete agreement he'd signed with Utah IT.

If he were willing to breach that contract, what else would he compromise on?

The first few months of the YUITS/Mamabargains marriage were bliss.

Maybe my gut instinct was wrong.

In addition to signing for six months, we also hired them to create our iPhone and Android apps. These would make the shopping process much more streamlined, and placing an order much faster—a vital part of retail Ecommerce success. Our customers wanted a simple purchasing experience, so the exorbitant cost to us was worthwhile.

James offered reputable websites as evidence of his teams' experience. Though, we later learned that he was actually blood related to his biggest brag-worthy creation—a huge corporation that had sponsored the Olympics several years prior.

Our agreement with YUITS for the mobile apps promised an eight-week deadline. Since we'd signed the web maintenance contract with Damon, if we weren't satisfied with YUITS' work by the time the apps were completed, the website maintenance contract would be over with, enabling us to part ways.

When the three-month honeymoon was over, the nearly two-year nightmare began. The complaints from our lifeblood—our customers—poured in immediately.

"I can't get this item added to my shopping cart, the 'add to cart' button stopped working."

"I can't get the site to load, your website is so slow!"

"I added items to my cart, but the 'process order' button doesn't work!"

"The site won't let me add my credit card number so I can pay you!"

The financial implications began to rear their ugly heads. People wanted to order, but many couldn't. Our credibility was on the line, too.

It was virtually impossible to quantify the sheer volume of issues because many purchasers went elsewhere when they encountered a problem, not taking the time to report it. For every complaint voiced, that meant there were likely five more—unreported. To us, one customer with technical issues warranted time spent attempting a resolution.

And why wasn't the site loading consistently? Someone with a credit card in hand, ready to pay, but couldn't, would spell disaster for a company.

It spelled disaster for Mamabargains.

The phone calls with our IT team increased, the complaints became more frequent, my anxiety at an all time high. Instead of brainstorming and growing, Mamabargains was plagued by tech troubles. We were putting out fires rather than preventing them from happening to begin with—a job YUITS was hired for.

"Everything seems to be humming along just fine, Jessica," James would say.

"I think that's a user error." (In other words, he blamed the *customers*, saying that *they* were the ones who were at fault.)

"I'm not sure how that could happen, I'm loading the site just fine from my location, Jessica. Must be an anomaly." The anomalous behavior became the new normal.

"I can't explain the latency in site loading times, Jessica." (Translation: 'I have no idea why the site is slow to load, or not loading at all.')

"I'll be in my London office and unavailable for a week." (Translation: 'I'm hiding from you even though you pay me big bucks to fix this shit.')

It didn't take long to figure out that Damon was a professional gambler who had no technical experience before YUITS appointed him to the crucial role of Mamabargains Project Manager. James had left us in the hands of someone with inadequate capabilities and this twerp was now gambling with our livelihood.

Eight, nine, ten, eleven, twelve. By *thirteen* weeks later, Mamabargains had no completed apps. We were falling behind our competition. Zulily was larger than life, and Groupon was having a great year. Let's not even talk about Babysteals, because they always seemed to do so well. I'm sure their development teams were reputable. Ours was a fucking joke.

The accountability is mine. Because even though I didn't like them, and even though my gut warned me against it, I still hired the bastards.

For the first time in our history, Mamabargains' rising numbers were dwindling. These circular arguments with James and the dip in business meant sheer panic for me.

"It's anxiety, Jess, you need anti-anxiety meds. Try Zoloft," my doctor suggested.

These panic-attacks—chest constricting and tightening, unable to breathe—would leave me in the ER. I felt like I was having mini-strokes. They'd hook me up to the machines and put me through a battery of tests. Even though the doctors could see a small 'heart event', they couldn't put a name on it other than 'anxiety'.

While I felt like I was going to die an anxiety-ridden death, Stanford was worried because I'd forget to eat regularly. He'd call daily, just to remind me to eat lunch. He knew I'd sit in my office for sixteen hours straight, non-stop, sometimes forgetting even to take pee breaks. The employees would often remind me, too.

And I'd done my research on this Zoloft stuff, "Won't Zoloft take away my edge? Because I'm pretty fond of my edge," I'd say to the Doc.

"No, Jessica, it'll take away *the* edge, not *your* edge."

I was out of options. Zoloft it was. Edge or no edge, I needed something to help balance me. I was spiraling out of control and I couldn't take another panic-attack, or wake-up to find myself covered from head to toe in hives at completely random times.

My body was an angry, unhealthy cluster fuck.

I'd field customer technical error reports at all hours, personally dealing with almost every single one of them. Some nights there were two, other nights, nearly hundred or more of them. Some customers will definitely remember speaking to me at odd hours of the night—I'd conference in Gregg, and we'd try to resolve the issue as a team. Every conflict has a source, we just had to find it.

I was desperate to find the cause. The future of Mamabargains hanging by a very thin thread.

Gregg was beside himself as well. Even though he developed and wrote code, he wasn't a server guy. The two languages were as different as Russian and Latin. He was the first to admit where his deficiencies lay, and server code was just not his forte. It was clear that whatever was going on, it was going on *inside* the servers, *not* within his code.

My gut served me well over the years and was often a topic of conversation when we'd discuss the technical issues with YUITS.

"I trust Jessica's gut when she says something's wrong guys, you *need* to look into it more than you are. She knows this website more thoroughly than anyone on the planet," Gregg would say to YUITS.

"Jessica's gut hasn't failed us before, please listen to her," Stanford would plead.

As a business owner, you do it all. If you don't know how to do it, you learn. I learned bookkeeping and accounting, warehouse procedures, shipping and receiving, marketing, business management, human resources, customer service, sales, high level partnerships, and I was damn good at cleaning that toilet.

Server language, though, isn't easily learned. And we were out of time.

"Yeah, you're right, something is definitely off," James finally admitted one day.

Did he just...? Yes. He admitted out loud that something wasn't right. It's about fucking time! Now we're getting somewhere!

"I'm glad you finally see there are glaring problems here, so how do we fix it?" I asked, hoping to hear a full of enthusiasm Gregg-like 'nothing is impossible' reply.

Not even close.

"I have no idea. I don't know what's wrong, and I don't know how to fix it or what caused it," James said.

"We pay you well enough that you should be able to use your resources and get to the bottom of it, this isn't a process I should have to micromanage. I have customers to care for, and a staff to look after. At this rate, we are going to begin layoffs soon," I said to James. And he knew I was serious. He could see the numbers. We could all see the numbers and no amount of Zoloft could make them better.

It sounds counter-intuitive, but when our six months ended with YUITS, we let it roll into the next six months. I didn't like it one bit, but after more than six months of waiting, our apps were still not done. James had us by our balls. I couldn't sever the contract with him while our apps were still incomplete—I'd invested thousands and thousands of dollars into them. Plus, there was an ongoing problem and I just knew we could fix it. Starting from scratch with yet another new team would stop us in our tracks.

James was finally acknowledging there was an issue, and sometimes admitting there's a problem is the first step in resolving it, right? Apparently this James fellow had other ideas.

The problem wasn't a secret any longer (Because I've got a pretty big mouth).

Customers began vocally complaining on Facebook (I wouldn't expect less).

Vendors began asking questions (We took longer than normal to pay them in full).

Our employees began wondering what was going on (They could see the stress fractures on my forehead).

The numbers didn't slowly dwindle. They were plummeting at a rate I'd never considered a possibility. It didn't seem real for this to be happening. I was in denial. I'd wake up and feel, for a fleeting moment, that it was all just a bad dream.

But it was a nightmare I couldn't actually wake up from.

Six months. Seven months. We'd been with YUITS for over a year, and our apps that were supposed to take eight weeks hit the eight months and counting mark—with no end in sight.

Mamabargains crashed weekly. Traffic was down. *Way* down. How was it possible that we now only had a quarter of the site traffic that we'd enjoyed in our first two years? We'd crashed just once when we were partnered with Procter and Gamble, now we were crashing regularly, with *less* traffic? How was it possible that at 2am, when the site had little to no visitors, it would take a shit?

The Procter and Gamble partnership ended, and with it, so did the monthly revenue—all reinvested into Mamabargains. There was no problem-solving money left.

Worst of all, the stress and anxiety-inducing headache that Mamabargains was becoming had bled into our personal lives. Stanford and I fought daily. Our kids could see and feel the tension. It was constant conflict.

"Something is so wrong here—these guys are fucking us over, Stanford. I don't trust them."

"Just give them time to work through it, Jessica, they'll figure it out," more patient Stanford would say.

"At what cost?" I'd shout. "We have to sell your truck."

"What? Are you serious?"

"Yes, Stan. We own the truck outright and payroll is due to be paid in two weeks. At this point, our sales are bringing in less than when we were two months old. The difference is that we aren't in our basement with no overhead. We have a staff of over twenty employees, contractors and consultants. We cannot sustain long-term like this. We need the money to pay the employees. We need to keep the business going while YUITS figures out what the fuck is wrong!"

But Stanford didn't need my explanation. He knew I was right—the words were just noise. Our family livelihood was relying on us figuring out this technical nightmare.

The truck was sold, and the money we made paid for *one* payroll period.

Next came the retirement account loan (which we are still paying on today).

We took the maximum allowed. It's what families do when it's time for them to send a child to college, or pay for a wedding, or help with medical expenses. We'd used it for Mamabargains. We paid vendors with it. We paid payroll with it. We paid our warehouse rent with it. We bought toilet paper for the office with it.

I hope my kids don't ever need braces.

We tried to avoid the potential of having to do layoffs. Who would we choose?

The single mom going to school every day after work to make a better life her daughter? Maybe the mom in sales with two daughters and an abusive husband at home? Should we lay off the dad with seven children? Which one of these loyal, long-time employees would we shaft first? We couldn't survive without them. We wouldn't be where we were without them. How would we make these terrible choices? Put the names in a hat and just draw one?

But then, how much longer could we put off the inevitable?

At what point should we call it quits?

We didn't have a penny left in savings—we had nowhere left to borrow from.

Don't touch the kids' savings accounts. Don't you dare.

We didn't have local family or friends supporting us. We were alone.

Stanford and I no longer spoke to each other, we shouted. Our weekly sushi dates dried up too. We couldn't afford them anymore. Our one and only sacred day a week where we could reconnect had to be cut from our routine. Goodbye, tuna. Sayonara, salmon.

I stopped paying myself regularly. Some months we'd do just okay, and I'd pay myself enough to buy groceries or make the car payment. I was working for less than minimum wage, considering the excess of hours I was putting in. Our credit cards were maxed. Our retirement account loan payment alone was more than we spent in groceries each month.

"I can't wait to be running Mamabargains someday, mom!" My oldest would tell me. Meanwhile, our accountant would say, "Jessica, there isn't enough money to cover the vendor payments this week."

Where Mamabargains began 'in the black' (profitable) and continued such for five years, it had now dipped its little toe into the red (negative, owing money).

Mamabargains was officially sprinting down the track of failure. And although James admitted there was a problem, he still couldn't work out how to fix it. Probably because our project manager was a professional gambler, *not* a tech guru, or perhaps because James was cold, calculating and un-caring.

Just a thought.

"James, do you realize what's at stake, here?"

"Yes, but to be honest, it's not my concern. I don't know what's wrong with the site. It probably has something to do with Gregg's coding". He said.

"James, it's *not* Gregg's coding. Everything was *fine* until *YUITS* came on board. Within three months of YUITS on staff, things began to go downhill, and not slowly, either," I'd tell him, only the Zoloft standing between he and an epic Jessica explosion of nuclear proportions. "It just doesn't make sense that sometimes I can't even get my own website to load. And customers complain constantly of the same issue. You can't blame Gregg's coding, or another 'anomaly'. This is *killing* us!" I'd say, blood boiling over.

"If at least 80% of your customers can access your site at any given time, than to me, there's no problem," he'd reply.

Comparing our numbers to what they were three months before YUITS came on board, they'd been more than double. That should've been proof enough. But James was busy pointing fingers anywhere except his own team. He'd say our customers were idiot moms (yes, his actual words). He'd claim Gregg had poor coding (his coding worked perfectly before YUITS). Challenging my scrutiny, in his obnoxious defensiveness, James would regularly call me 'overly sensitive'.

Oh. I'm sorry—does my concern for my crumbling business (at your hands) and customer experience bother you, James? Does my on-point gut terrify you? Are you actually biting the hand that feeds you?

"Man-up and take some damn accountability!" I'd say.

"Again, it's simply not my problem, Jessica," he'd defensively fire back.

Disgruntled customers were leaving Mamabargains in hordes.

And our competitors, whose websites and apps worked seamlessly, were siphoning off of our failures.

Stanford returned to his full time job as an engineer (to his relief!). The stressful daily burden of proving the coding issues was left to Gregg and I. It was our mission to get to the bottom of what was ailing Mamabargains. Whatever was causing the disease—we'd need to figure it out. We were resourceful—we could do it.

I'd just put on my happy, fake-face every day, confident we'd sort it all out eventually.

Or was that the Zoloft talking, and we were actually just fucked?

Was I becoming more like my dad at the peak of his illness?

Could that happen to me...?

What's with these voices in my head?

Something I learned a long time ago in business *and* in life, is that 80% of customers—people in general—want only 20% of your time, while the other 20% will *try* to poach the other 80%. The trick is give less to those stealing the most from you.

I hope that Kevin might, just for a moment, think back to what he did to me, and feel a little regret. But you know what? I don't *regret* that it happened.

I am no victim. It was a painful, life-altering experience, but I chose to make it as positive as I could. Sure, at first it destroyed me just a little bit.

Although I hated him for it, I forgave Kevin a long time ago. I'll never forget how powerless and helpless it made me feel, or how angry I was for being objectified by him. I felt dirty and ashamed, like I'd 'asked' for it, which, of course I didn't. He didn't *make* me feel a particular way, he didn't *force* me to be angry, I *let* myself be angry.

I've known rape victims who, like me, celebrate how strong it made them. Women (and men) who've let go of the baggage that was left in the wake of their violation. Find the good. Find a way to take control back, because until you do—whoever did that horrible thing to you *wins*. They *still* have power over you.

The seven stages of grief took over my life for a while after the rape. I was lost somewhere in the depression phase. Drowning in my loneliness, I found Jake, the poet later turned druggie. He brought me out of my 'plain Jane librarian' persona. The new Jess provided an energy and strength I didn't know I had in me. He did that for me. See? There's a silver lining on every black cloud—even when the clouds name is Jake.

At barely twenty-one years young, I found a small hole in the wall 'club' in downtown Tacoma. A dance club with a cage and a bar in the corner of the main dance floor. This was no Ritz Carlton, and the cage wasn't for the out of line patrons or wild animals.

It's also the last place on Earth you'd expect to find little miss librarian Jessica.

Darling Jake said to me, "You'd make a great dancer. You have such a slender, sexy body. I'd love it if you took up dancing, but for money. I seriously doubt you could do it. I don't think you have the guts."

Excuse me, Asshole? You dare doubt me? A week later I was interviewing at the local nightclub. I was a shoe-in with my big size zero waist. My job title? Pole Dancer.

There was one, well, technically, two *small* issues, according to the club owner. "Your tits are a little, well, they're a little on the *little* side."

"They are what they are, and I'm not getting a boob job, so you and your customers can take 'em or leave 'em," I replied.

"I'll give you a chance if you go into the back, meet the other girls and head out onto the floor. You can go first."

"What? You want me to dance, like, now, tonight?"

"Yes. Yes, I do" he said with a sly smile. I half expected to see some gold popping out from behind that toothy grin, but no luck, just bright, unusually straight whites gleaming out from behind his pencil thin lips. I think he doubted me too.

Heart pumping, I was mortified, but kind of excited too. I'm not so sure I'd *ever* had an adrenaline rush quite like that before. Meeting the other girls and getting ready for my first ever stage dance was nerve-wracking. Luckily there was a nice girl that let me use her G-string. I mean, she *looked mostly* clean, but so did the captain of our High School football team, and he gave crabs to half the cheerleaders—so—yeah.

The pasties—*nipple covers*—came next. All the dancers were required to wear them. They didn't leave much to the imagination, either. They seemed pointless unless you were doing some callback to Madonna's cone boob days.

The club was loud, and since I'd come in to interview before it opened for the night, it was also overly empty. I suppose that made me feel a little better—I'd only be dancing for a crowd of less than ten men. The early bird gets the worm, right?

I'd done gymnastics, how hard could this pole-dancing thing be? Dad would be so proud. Those days practicing on his homemade balance beam—they'd finally paid off.

The advice from the girls? "Grab the pole, spin around, and fuck the thing."

Well? Okay. I'll just—have sex with the pole, then. What could possibly go wrong?

Turns out I'd forgotten an essential ingredient to a successful, non-burning pole encounter. Baby oil or baby powder. I wish the girls had warned me, because now I had a battle wound—a totally manageable, but embarrassing inner thigh pole burn.

But I made $11 that first dance!

Business brain took over and I did the math. I'd made $11 for four minutes of thigh-burning grinding on a metal pole. That meant if I worked only for an hour and made that admittedly measly amount per dance, I'd walk away with $165—cold hard cash. Multiply that by the two nights a week, over the course of a month? Minus the baby oil, powder and my own pasties? I'd still take home around $1,300! Not bad for a side gig (with a touch of thigh burn) taking up a whole eight hours of my life per month.

Sweet, that $11 I made will pay for half a tank of gas. That's $8 more than I had to my name when I walked in.

Credit Union employee by day, shady shit-hole pole dancer by night. I worked there religiously twice a week. I'd get up in the morning, put on my suit and go work at the prim and proper day job. "Welcome to Rainier Credit Union, how can I help you?"

I was an inexperienced kid trying to make her drug-dealing man-whore of a boyfriend happy. Jake didn't show for my first official night on the job—or any night after. I wondered why, especially after he'd been so persistent in the first place.

I thought, maybe I could own this club, someday.

Shut up. You don't want a strip club! What's wrong with you?

Sure, while I was up on the pole with a G-string wedgie from hell stuck in my ass crack and pasties literally *glued* to my boobs, I *appeared* to be just like any other fucked-up, drug-head pole-dancer out there. In reality, I was gaining life experience and street smarts the hard way—the way most girls my age would have run a million miles from. Plus—the nights there were nights away from Jake.

Naturally, the reasonable, levelheaded Credit Union employee in me was terrified someone I knew would visit the club and recognize me. My day job was about twenty miles away, but small towns *do* talk. I was certain that the credit union janitor frequented these types of places. Just a guess—he *did* look like some of the creepers that gave me tips.

I'd be mortified if one of my Credit Union customers or coworkers showed up.

What if my brothers—or worst of all—my *dad* came in? "I owe my gymnastics and dancing skills to a man in the audience tonight, thanks for the balance beam, Dad, this next one's for you!"

I worked in his palace of a place for just over a month. My stint as a dancer ended with me no-call no-showing to one of my shifts—because I couldn't take the drool anymore. And my profit calculations were *a bit* off. I took home over $2000 that month.

But I'd grown tired of washing the dirty dancing money I made nightly in my bathroom sink back at home. Trying to hide wet money from druggie Jake, I'd wash it, and then tuck it under the bathroom rug while it dried nice and flat. He never cleaned, so I wasn't remotely worried he'd find it. Yes, I was money laundering, on a very small, completely literal, legal scale.

Watching all those nasty older men salivating over the women in this club was something I just couldn't take. I was scared shitless to even do a lap-dance. I just couldn't imaging getting my Lady Down South all up in Old Man Martin's (a regular) Snake in His Pants while I pretended it was Leonardo DiCaprio I was grinding on.

My co-workers were colorful and eclectic. One girl, whose stage name was Trixie (her real name was Melissa), was a single mom going to school to get her GED. Her grandma was raising her son while she danced at night and worked two other jobs during the day. That girl could rock the house. She was the most requested dancer. Men *and* women loved lap dances from her. I sat in on a few of them, watching and learning. I'm pretty positive her clitoris was made of gold.

My dancer name was Daphne. Actually, at first it was Daffy. Because they made me choose the name on the spot, only moments before I was to walk onto stage, and I was thinking about Daisy Duck, but blurted out Daffy instead. Oops.

Thus, the DJ called out "Now we welcome little hottie, Daffy. Tonight is her first dance, ever." I don't know what was more funny, the fact that I'd somehow chosen to be named after a duck, or the fact that my glued on pasties were about to fall off the whole dance. They thought I was grabbing my boobs, instead I was trying to reaffix the damn pasties. Later, the club manager made me change my stupid name. He said the name Daffy reminded him of a cartoon character. Wonder why?

The birth of Daphne had materialized from a duck.

There was another woman who went by the name 'Crystal'. She looked to be in her fifties, but was in her thirties—and clearly a meth addict. I never understood how men could be attracted to a pimple-laden, crater-faced woman who had bleeding scabs on her face and chipped/cracked/rotting teeth from her years of meth use. She told me she was married at one time and had 'lots of kids' but that she couldn't remember how many kids she actually had. Never caught her real name, but found it amusing that her stage name was Crystal and her drug of choice was meth. I'm not sure if she had a sense of humor, because she only ever said these few words to me:

"I got lots of dem kids. Like a real lots, but I ain't member esatly how meny." Crystal terrified me. I crossed my fingers that at the stroke of midnight, I wouldn't turn into her, a tweeker by association.

I never believed a word she said. I was dating Jake, a drug addict, and therefore had learned pretty quick that most of what comes out of an addict's mouth is bullshit. I'd just nod and smile, never taking my eyes off her black and brown teeth. Is that food? No, no, it's just tooth rot.

Mr. Absent was apparently using the time that I was away at 'work' to fuck some other girl(s). I only walked in on him once, in my bed, at our tiny rental house. At that exact moment, Jake was jizzing onto Gloria's face and I can't believe I didn't bitch slap that whore right then and there. Instead, I told her, *"Get out of the house I pay the rent for. While you're at it, take the disgusting fuck-face you just screwed with you."* Because I'm a lover, not a fighter. In actuality, I said that only in my head. I couldn't talk like that around Jake, he'd punch me if I did—or worse.

She wasn't even cute. She looked like a llama trapped in an elephant's body. Long neck, short, stout body. Probably would've spit at me too, but I kept my distance.

She grabbed her stuff and huffed past me, cracking a huge smile. Her teeth were also rotted out. Probably a friend of Crystal's.

Jake laughed at me, grabbed some of his stuff and vanished for a few days. "Don't let your fucking forty of Mickey's hit you in the head and kill you on the way out, you piece of shit!" I shouted as he tore out of the driveway in his stupid hoop-d gangsta Cadillac with Dayton rims on hydraulics. Words were all I had to use against him, even if I said them out of earshot, I still said them.

Dancing taught me, if nothing else, to defend myself. It taught me to stand up for myself and to be strong.

By then, the on and off again Jake/Jessica groundhog day relationship that had become a horrifying nightmare was moving to its end-times, and I'm glad that he strengthened my resolve with his cheating, lying ways—elephant-llama crack whore or not.

Dancing was a way to say, "Fuck you world, I can do whatever I choose. Fuck you, Jake, for telling me that you wished I'd try it but didn't think I had enough guts to. Don't tell me I don't have guts. I've got guts, and I'll shit them all over your face when you see I'm doing exactly what you thought I wasn't capable of accomplishing."

Yes, I've just said that pole dancing was an *accomplishment* of mine. In a screwed up little way, it was a goal I set and accomplished. Someone didn't believe that I could do it, so I proved that asshole wrong.

Dad sick at home, me living in Tacoma, I needed a way out. Working at the Credit Union was less than I'd imagined, and even though it was a good job, I continued to dream of someday owning my own business. I needed to get out of Washington.

January 25th, 1999. I was on the phone with a customer and alone behind the teller line at the Credit Union when I looked up to see four dreamy guys approaching my counter. "Diane, I'll have to call you back later, four really good looking guys just walked in."

"Lucky you," said Diane, who was clearly not a psychic.

I hung up, approached my window, and walked up to the former dreamy customer now nightmarish robber who was wearing a black glove—and he was pointing his gun directly at my face.

Was he wearing that glove when he walked in? Why didn't I notice that? Is this really happening?

He paced a navy blue backpack onto my counter.

"Fill it up. Put all the money in the bag. Now!"

The emergency button was under my counter—*if I could just get to it without being obvious.* No, that wouldn't work. I'd have to wait until the right moment, otherwise he'd see me for sure.

His eyes were piercingly blue and beautiful.

Why isn't he wearing a mask? Why are none of them wearing masks?

It didn't matter, because I only saw those blue eyes. Oh, and his dirty blonde hair. I was silently pleading with those blue eyes to spare me. This wasn't the way I wanted to go out, defending a Credit Union's money in a shitty little town in Washington.

There's more to life than this, Jessica. You'll get through this. Hopefully...

I filled the backpack as demanded, and turned to walk away as he stepped back from my counter. I was hoping that was the extent of the robbery. I'd momentarily forgotten about his accomplices, but they were busy sticking to their carefully laid plan.

I'd noticed one of them holding the loan officers at gunpoint in the corner office while another stood guard at the front door. That's two of them, three including the guy who approached me first. I was certain I'd seen four enter the building. I noticed there was a customer sitting in her car at the drive-up teller window. *Look up, lady. Please look up from that deposit slip.* But she was unaware of the drama unfolding inside, never catching a glimpse of our 'black-clad robbers' (as the newspaper later dubbed them) who didn't even wear black, other than the gloves.

Looking away from the drive-through, I was immediately met with the barrel of *another gun.* He held it only an inch from my nose. *This* guy seemed to enjoy the exhilaration of holding my life in his hand as much as the *first* guy had. *Just grab the gun, Jess, you can do it. You are strong.* This guy wore dark brown corduroy pants. His shoes were scuffed and brown, his cerulean green eyes matched his pale skin perfectly.

These guys weren't young—they were just kids, teenagers, twenty max.

Don't do it, remember your training. Give them what they want. Let them leave. Life before the money, that's what they taught us.

I was made to empty the teller drawer at the drive-through window into his bag. They had two total drawers of money in their bags, surely that was enough?

As I was thinking about how I'd escape, the one that'd robbed me first briskly approached.

"What's behind *that?*" he shouted, pointing to the huge metal door behind me.

I froze.

I was alone, completely isolated behind the teller line, no one there to help me.

"Um, that's the vault," I responded, voice shaking.

"Good, open it," he said, his voice chillingly calm.

I still hadn't pressed the emergency button. There wasn't an opportunity, and now it was yards away.

I had no choice in that chilling moment because I had two guns pointed at me. The thing is, though, vaults are not easy things to open even at the best of times. They require two keys, and the keys must be put into the locks simultaneously and turned in unison.

Then there is the combination once you open the locks.

And there are two of those.

No one ever goes into the vault room alone, there's always 'dual control'. It takes two people to operate two locks, and two combinations.

Lucky me, I had the two sets of keys and knew both combinations by heart because I was the lead teller on shift that day. I was still *only one* person. One trembling, terrified person who could hardly think straight on account of the two guns pointed at my head.

Diane on the phone was right. Lucky me.

The other two tellers were still in the back on their break.

Maybe they could see this unfolding on the screens that broadcasted the video from the front of the Credit Union?

Were they calling the cops? If they don't see it, I hope they don't walk in on this scene.

Spinning a combination lock as you have guns in your face is no easy feat. And I choked.

One try. No luck.

Two tries. No luck.

And the more I failed, the more I fumbled and shook and thought I was going to get a bullet to the brain.

The robbers held the cold steel of their gun barrels against my temples.

"OPEN. THE. VAULT. BITCH. OR. I. *WILL.* KILL. YOU."

Oh. The vault. Why didn't you just say so, silly? I can totally do that for you!

When people say that their life flashes before their eyes, they speak truth.

As I was about to die, in that crappy little credit union, a short lifetime of memories washed over me. Some I didn't even realize were that important. I had visions of people that meant nothing to me (but who left me with important experiences), as well as people who I loved. I saw my parents, my grandparents and brothers. I saw single-mom Trixie—er, Melissa, from the nightclub, I saw my best friend, Elizabeth (I was going to miss her). I thought of Jake, and even of Kevin. I saw Marie, the friend who abandoned me, and I thought of the baby that was once in my belly that I'd never know.

And I said goodbye to them all in that pre-death, frozen slice of time.

I was convinced I'd die because I'd never get those combinations right.

But then... Holy Mother of a God I'm not sure I believe in!

The vault unlocked. I'd done it. I somehow opened the thing.

The robbers emptied the vault, including the bait money that was inside. *We have all of those serial numbers documented, you idiots. Have fun spending that.*

The rest of that morning was a blur. They fled the branch, and as I came out of the vault, I jumped to push the emergency button like it was my sole mission in life.

I fell to the floor—in shock. I don't remember them arriving, but when they did, the EMT's put an oxygen mask on me, loaded my limp body onto the gurney and away we went.

Twenty-three minutes passed from the moment the robbers walked into the Credit Union that morning to when I was wheeled out of the branch. Twenty-three minutes that felt like hours of my life.

A week later, I tried to go back to work. I tried and I failed. I just couldn't do it. It marked the first anxiety attack I ever suffered. Just because I wasn't at work, didn't mean I could simply forget the terrible incident.

The FBI agent on the case rigorously interrogated me because my boyfriend was a drug dealer, and they knew he had a rap sheet a mile long. Guys, he's not *that* smart. As much as I *loathe* him, he had no part of this. I don't talk about my bank job, and he doesn't ask. He's too busy snorting coke for eight days straight to orchestrate a robbery. And he doesn't hang out with good-looking guys like my robbers, either. He hangs out with crack heads.

There were binders of mug shots I had to thumb through and a lineup I'd eventually have to attend. Not long after the robbery, a disgruntled associate they owed drug money to, called and snitched. He reported that the four guys had moved to Miami, Florida, and were blowing the cash rapidly on drugs, women, and a sweet apartment on the beach.

The money from the robbery only lasted six months. When it ran out, the four idiots had to take a bus home to Washington because they really *did* spend every last dime. All four were arrested at the bus depot in Seattle as they stepped off their end-of-the-road party wagon.

I was too terrified to stay at work. I quit, not able to bring myself to walk into another bank for the next seven years. The credit union near-death experience rocked my world.

Months later I was finally given a court date, one for each of the assailants.

I had to explain four different times in court how the robbery personally impacted me. I was made to watch surveillance video of the robbery *four* times. I watched myself crumble to the floor moments before the ambulance guys came to load me onto that gurney—*four* times. It's a memory I only have because I saw it unfold on video.

It was the robbery that just kept on giving.

On the last day of court hearings, the judge brought all four criminals into court. Since they'd robbed us together, they'd be sentenced together, the judge explained.

And what did the sons-of-bitches get for all this life-changing heartache?

Five years.

That was it—the legal requirement in Washington State to charge them for bringing a gun into a federal institution. Even though they'd held guns to my head in the vault. Even after the entire courtroom watched two of them on video pointing a gun at my face, threatening my life, all they got was five lousy years.

I'd never be the same. It was just another 'experience' in my younger years that helped shape me into the woman I was meant to become someday.

I decided that day that I'd never back down when I saw something I wanted, or deserved—that I wouldn't let a bank robbery, druggie boyfriend, rape, sick dad, ex-best friends, or religion define me.

I had to get out of Washington.

That was my plan, at least.

'Hire slow, fire fast'.

Why?

Because it's not a matter of *if* an employee is going to steal from you, it's *when*, how much, and how often. You know, those stolen pens all add up. That's why you haven't gotten a raise—your boss knows you steal seventeen of them a week.

Mamabargains had reached great heights, but every day was a battle—stress, falling income, and shitty technical problems. I tried not to give into the constant feeling of impending doom, but it was a nearly impossible feat—especially when I had employees to think of. Let's not forget my own family.

The YUITS issues destroying our bottom line topped my kill list—a relentless life distraction. Problem resolution infected our lives every second I could spare, and every second I couldn't.

We were hemorrhaging money, soon it'd be staff. I'd upped my Zoloft dose, second-guessing every decision and instinct. The anxious drugged-up funk became my new reality—Jessica the Zoloft Zombie.

Our office environment became as toxic as our servers.

As if I wasn't busy enough with the torture of technical tribulations, now I'd have to prepare for the latest hurricane on the horizon—the impending doom of employee drama. I'd grown a pair of cojones in the time YUITS was with us and it was time to put them to good use finding the source of this new office disease working its way through the staff.

Becca was barely twenty-one. She'd say to anyone that'd listen, (because, yes, she was still living at home with mommy and daddy), "I'm going to ride this parent train for as long as possible." I was caught in the middle because Becca's mom, Karen, was also a good friend of mine. She'd ask me, "Am I ruining Becca by spoiling her so much?"

'No shit, Sherlock! You're destroying her chance at independence by silver-plating her!' But I wasn't about to tell Karen how to raise her daughter. There's that rule somewhere about never, ever criticizing someone's parenting techniques. What Becca really needed was a parent, but what she had in Karen was more of a co-dependent cash cow *disguised* as a mom. And I was too busy to play mommy to her spoiled little brat.

I've mentioned Becca before in a positive light, because despite her being an entitled ass-wipe millennial, she really did do great things for Mamabargains before she went off the rails. She'd been super with the customers, and great with the vendors.

My mistake was letting Becca get too close. I took her on one too many sushi dates and gave her one too many raises and far too many bonuses. I granted Becca too much freedom and too many requested days off. I'd done it all because I considered Becca more than a co-worker, and more than a friend. I treated her like the sister I always yearned for.

Trouble in paradise wasn't far off.

"Hey, Becca? When you do supply ordering, are you using the Visa or MasterCard?" CFO Stanford asked. Chief *Financial* Officers have a right to know how and where money is being spent.

"What? Of *course* I use the Visa! You think I'm *dumb*? You *told* me to use the Visa, so I *use* the Visa. Don't question my integrity!" was Becca's snippy out of left-field answer.

He wasn't questioning her integrity—at least not *that* day. But since she thought he was, it suggested things were, in fact, more complicated than they'd seemed on the surface. Guilty people do bizarre things.

"It was just a question, Becca. There's a supply order showing up on the MasterCard statement, and you're the one in charge of supply ordering, that's all," soothed my peace-loving husband.

Stanford hadn't been to the office in a few weeks, so he hadn't noticed Becca's rapid decline in attitude and performance the way I had. Plus, he wasn't exactly proficient in dealing with HR troubles.

Becca was suddenly callous toward everything and everyone at Mamabargains. I'd ask her if she was okay and she'd give me a brush-off response like, "I'm fine, Jess. Just stressed with school," or, "I'm okay, just having relationship issues."

When he got home, Stanford told me what happened, "I don't know what's going on with Becca, but something's up. That behavior can't happen again without her getting written up. She crossed a line today."

The next day, I spoke to Becca privately and explained that she couldn't speak to management, or anyone else like that again at Mamabargains. It wasn't the first time she'd belittled someone in management—but I'd make damn sure it was the last.

Two days later, she put in her *one-week* notice. "It's not you, it's me," her resignation letter said, and "I need to focus more on school." Even without a two-week notice, I was ready to rip that soiled Becca-bandage off. I should've sent her packing the same day, but feared backlash from Karen, my friend—her mom.

We unraveled in every direction. It was all coming to a head, and while I thought this staff crisis might be our undoing, I was wrong. Becca leaving Mamabargains wasn't our unraveling, but the stench she left behind really took me to the edge.

Breathe, Jess. You're drowning. Could someone just throw me a rope, already?

YUITS wasn't helping matters. They were less and less available. And we were paying them the same asinine rate while they dodged our calls. Customer complaints peaked.

Tightening. It's tightening. The chest constricting pain is back. Isn't Zoloft supposed to prevent these anxiety attacks? Isn't it supposed to help keep me relaxed?

I couldn't breathe and there was the new, 'I can't feel my face' symptom. The doctor increased the Zoloft dosage by another quarter of a pill. I was up to two pills a day and all it was doing was turning me into a zoned-out, dead-CEO walking.

Becca's post-mortem poison hit us more venomously than when she was our employee. The pandemic infected two of my employees who were still friends with her. Jane and Hailey morphed into Becca with their chip on the shoulder attitudes and shitty work ethics to go right alone with it.

"How are you liking it here, Jane?" I asked one afternoon.

"Oh, I love it here," she said with monotonous sarcasm.

"Hailey, how about I buy you two lunch today?" I asked, sensing their unease.

"Oh, sure!" Hailey said, clearly only interested in free lunch.

At the sushi bar, the three of us sat in silence. I used the restroom and returned to see them laughing their asses off. As I approached, the deafening silence resumed.

The awkward lack of conversation meant I could think about the YUITS issues. I really didn't have the time to try and decrypt their odd employee behavior.

One evening, after Hailey and Jane clocked out after their shift, I sat down at their computers to lock each of them down. Nothing out of the ordinary, because they'd left them on—again—per their usual, posing a security threat. A simple office rule that they'd *rarely* followed.

Unfortunately, I'm a nosy fuck.

Fortunately, I view my curiosity as 'intelligence gathering.'.

If, for instance, you leave yourself logged into Facebook on a computer that *I* pay for, and you chat on said computer while collecting a paycheck from *me* to *work*—at the desk *I* bought, in *my* office, I have a right to be nosy.

The instant Facebook message on Hailey's screen read: "Is bitch still there?"

I wonder who bitch is supposed to be? Me?

So I clicked 'open'. Admit it, you'd do the same.

I'd nosy-snoopered my way into a more than six-month message chain between Becca, Hailey and Jane.

And, it was soul-destroying.

"Stanford thinks he owns this place. I own this place. He's clueless," messaged Becca, a few minutes after her run-in with my husband that day over the office supplies.

She was on the clock when she typed it.

"Take the employee discount code and give it to whoever you want, if Jessica asks, just tell her the person that used it is your sister. She'll never know." It was reserved for employees and immediate family of our employees. A privilege I'd given them all. A discount on already heavily discounted items. Go figure.

"She's standing right in front of me. I wish she'd take that ugly baby and go home!" Becca had written several weeks prior. Because you know, I'd had my third baby boy three weeks prior and was bringing him to work with me, because that's what owners do—in my world, that's called dedication and sacrifice.

"I hate this place," Jane messaged at one point. "I'm getting out of here, make sure to clock me out in a few hours," Becca added. In my world, that's called *stealing*.

"She's so stupid. I told her I needed Tuesdays off for school. Instead, I'm going home to have sex with Mike (some guy that *wasn't* her boyfriend—so she admitted to cheating *in writing* too—this is getting good!).

"She's clueless," Hailey wrote. And I was.

"She's stupid," Becca wrote. To hire her, *yes*—*very* stupid.

"She'll never know how much we've stolen from her!" Becca wrote, Jane and Hailey added a smiley face emoticon. The image deepened my pain. And she was right. I'd never know *exactly* how much they stole from us.

This chain of traitorous assassinations between the three girls went on and on. I'd done so much for not just Becca, but I'd opened my heart to all three of them, taking them in, giving them responsibility, mentoring them, giving them raises, bonuses, paying them for their hard work.

And I'd been stabbed in the back in return. I never realized I was paying them for deception. That wasn't in their job descriptions.

Stanford stood next to me, reading over my shoulder.

He placed his hand on top of mine, which was glued to the mouse, ferociously scrolling, reading, scrolling, crying, scrolling—the physical pain in my heart unbearable.

"That's enough! *Stop* reading it. Just screenshot it, email it to yourself, and copy the attorney. Print it out. Let's go *home*, our kids need us. I've had enough. You don't deserve this, Jess." Stanford's voice was stern, anger boiling over.

I looked up at him, with tears rushing down my flushed cheeks, "I wonder how *much* they stole? The financial burden could break us, Stanford—I have to find out how much. Why? I'm so confused. Is this a *joke*?"

Why did I trust them? Why do I trust people? What the fuck is wrong with me?

Becca had always insisted on staying in control of payroll. Each time we tried to turn the payroll over to our bookkeeper, Becca would say, "No, it's totally fine. I really like doing payroll, it's part of my job and I'd really like to keep doing it." Now it appeared I'd mistaken her dedication and loyalty, for something much more sinister.

The next morning, I called our payroll processing company.

I had three stacks in front of me.

One stack contained the Facebook chat chain with dates and times.

The other had the actual time clock punches from the same period of time.

The last one was the doozy—the smoking gun. It was the ledger of hours that Becca *called* into the payroll company for each time period during her disgruntled Facebook chat timeframe.

I busted her. At least there was *one* mystery I was able to figure out.

What she *called into payroll* vs. what was *manually logged* into the time clock on the wall in our office differed. Those punched hours were inaccurate because her good friend Hailey was clocking her out long after she left for the day—their Facebook chat chain acknowledged that fact on various occasions.

And I signed off on it—all of it—because I trusted her. I *never* double-checked or cross-referenced the amount of hours she (or in this case, Hailey) 'worked' with the hours she actually called into the payroll company.

Becca, my prized employee, stole *at least* ninety-four hours of overtime that we could prove. I instinctively knew there were more, but didn't have the energy to dig for more transgressions.

YUITS issues took precedence.

They are damaging your livelihood. Fire the fuckers! Fire all of them!

The next day came to a close with Hailey and Jane the only two employees left in the office. My heart raced because I knew that firing people was never easy. I was never great at it, but had gotten better over the years. Confidently, I approached Hailey and Jane, who were giggling at their desks in the corner.

Is this Junior High? These girls and their secretive giggling— juvenile fucking delinquents need to learn a lesson.

"Hey, did you two know that we monitor our computers?" Hailey looked at me like a deer in headlights. Big, huge, wide-open eyes, her mouth stayed shut. She was clearly at a loss for words, which spoke volumes.

And by *monitor*, I conveniently failed to mention the word *snoop*, because let's be honest, here—that's what I actually did. But *that* was none of their business. Those were *my* computers and *my* livelihood they'd fucked with. Monitor—snoop—same difference!

Jane looked up from her computer, full attention on me.

"You're aware that anything you do on the computers, we can actually see? That includes 'chat' rooms, instant messaging, Facebook, emails—and that's because your computers are *our* computers."

"Uh, yeah, of course. But we wouldn't be doing anything that would cause concern, so yeah. Um, why are you bringing this up, Jess?" Hailey asked. I was impressed—she really was a *spectacular* liar.

Enough small talk—cut to the chase!

"Have either of you *ever* participated in shit talking Stanford and I while on the clock *in this office*? And if so, have you done so on *our* computers?"

Even though I read admittance to their indiscretions with my own eyes, I was wondering how much they'd lie or if they'd actually admit their wrongdoing?

Even though the confrontation was justified, I was nervous. It was a different type of adrenaline rush than pole dancing, or watching the sales on an item go from one order to eight hundred orders within ten minutes flat. I was losing my nerve. I could see them squirming in their seats, too. Would they get up and run out of the office? Call me some of the things to my face that they'd been cowardly messaging behind my back?

Mean people always have more confidence with the anonymity of sitting behind their keyboards and I'd blown these callous bitches' anonymity.

Hailey completely melted down. She began sobbing uncontrollably and finally blurted out, "I'm *so sorry*, Jess." I wasn't sure how to react. I hadn't expected an emotional apology. I'd expected them to both huff out of the office and quit. I'd even spoken to a temp agency and lined up replacements for them for the following day.

Jane's apology immediately followed weeping Hailey's. It wasn't as emotional, but seemed just as heartfelt.

Why had they done these things? I needed an explanation, because it's not as if the crap talking lasted a few days, it'd been a months-long chain of venomous insults.

Because you're a fucking enabler. You always have been. You let people walk all over you, and you brush it under the rug.

"Why did you all do this?" I asked.

"We got sucked into Becca's drama. Her negativity was toxic and we just joined in as a way to feel like we fit in with her," was Hailey's explanation.

"I felt horrible, Jess, I really did. Becca trained me, and I felt torn," said Jane.

"Becca talked shit about you and Stanford my very first day," said Hailey, "She trained everyone to despise you, but never gave reasons why—I still don't know why."

My blood pressure was rising and I could feel another heart episode coming on.

"She said horrible things about you and Stanford and your family, but you're awesome owners—great role models," Jane offered. "You've been nothing but wonderful and generous to me *and* my family."

I just listened.

I was starting to feel bad for them. They were both raised to be good Mormon girls. Somehow I'd expected more of them. I was disappointed in myself for expecting more from their religious upbringing—after all, religion had disappointed me so many times before, why should these Mormon girls be any different? Religion would never prove to me to be anything but a sham, a mask worn to cover insecurities and fear, a scapegoat for poor behaviors—because God will always forgive you. But I might not.

I kept calm and professional, explaining that what I'd discovered in the message-chain was fraud, that it was theft. I told Hailey and Jane that our attorney advised us to prosecute *all three of them*. I had hundreds of pages of screenshots documenting the libel. Once something is in writing, it's permanent. I informed them that Facebook could be subpoenaed for the information directly, if that's what it took. They needed to see that I was serious, that this was serious—a crime.

I finished by saying that I needed the weekend to think about what I'd do about their lies. Despite their apologies, I didn't know if I wanted them to be a part of the Mamabargains' family anymore. I needed them to also think about whether or not they still wanted their jobs after this humiliation.

They both stared with tear-filled eyes, lost for words.

I went home that night and broke down. The hardened business owner, Jessica, who kept it together and hardly ever showed weakness, bawled her eyes out.

The experience was overwhelming. I couldn't stop thinking about how we'd worked our asses off to build Mamabargains. This was our livelihood and these girls were helping YUITS destroy it. On the other hand, they were young, and I knew first-hand that people can make mistakes. The next morning I'd have to deal with the issue one way or another. Part of me hoped Hailey and Jane wouldn't even show up. Another part of me was thinking they'd show some spine by respectfully resigning.

And then the site crashed—again. The night I needed to sleep the upset off, I was awake for four hours mercilessly urging our development team to find answers.

I walked into the office Monday morning, exhausted, and an hour later than usual.

I didn't want any other employees to know what was up.

I was disappointed to see that Hailey and Jane were both at their desks, working diligently. It looked like I'd have to be the one to make a decision.

I went into my office and Jane appeared almost immediately with an envelope in her hand, looking devastated.

"Jess, can I talk to you privately, please?" she said, closing my previously always open office door behind her.

Yes! She's going to resign!

She handed me the envelope with the resignation and I immediately complimented her on her courage, "I think you're making a good decision, Jane. Thank you".

"You should probably read what's inside, before you say anything," she replied, looking a bit taken aback.

The envelope please...

Inside was a card, no white space remaining, she'd written a heartfelt apology for her actions—her crimes. This was no resignation. Jane wanted to keep her job. She was sorry, determined to earn our trust back. I was overwhelmed with emotion and forgiveness.

We hugged, and even though I came so close to firing her that morning, I had a change of heart. Why? Because she was young, she'd screwed up, admitted it, and took accountability for her mistakes, for her part in it all. Everyone deserves a second chance. Everyone deserves forgiveness. Her apology earned her the opportunity to explain—because there are two sides to every story.

Hailey gave a similar verbal apology later that day, begging for mercy for her role in the drama that had unfolded.

I wrote them both up, holding them responsible for their part in the theft, and into their employee folders went the evidence, write-ups and apologies.

And I grew a little that day.

They both stuck with Mamabargains for at least another year after 'the incident'. More than anything, that should show that they truly loved their jobs, and that Becca was the real issue all along.

Despite keeping the incident a secret from Becca and her family, because I didn't want to mix business and personal, and because Hailey begged me not to tell her best friend what I'd discovered, it came out eventually, because lies will never stay buried.

The more than six-year friendship I'd had with Becca's mom, Karen, ended explosively and forever, months after the incident when Hailey and Becca had been drinking one night. Drunken Hailey told Becca everything, and horrified Becca scrambled, knowing that what I knew could destroy her, her relationships, and her job, all of it. Preempting the rumor mill, Becca went to her mom and claimed I was talking shit about *her*, telling people that she was a thief. As I'd expected, Karen, took Becca's side and told me she didn't want to see the cold, hard evidence. She didn't want to believe that all kids lie—especially hers.

Each of those girls have to live with the fact that they all not only thieved money from Mamabargains in the form of stolen hours and stolen employee discount codes, but they also destroyed friendships with their dishonesty. My guess is that they'll never forget what it felt like to be caught red-handed. The most painful part wasn't the scheister heisters, it was the fact that I hadn't made time for many friends over the years. The ones I'd made time for, like Karen, I'd valued. In the end, it was *me* that Karen didn't value.

And I had another regret.

It's too bad that in all the years we owned Mamabargains we were too busy to christen the place. Stanford and I should've bumped uglies on Becca's desk—on her keyboard and in her chair before she quit. I could've had silent revenge, reveling in our after-sex every time she touched our stuff and spewed her dysentery talk all over our computers.

Maybe I could've taken a shit in her smoothie blender she kept at her desk? That would've been the ultimate retribution. But, like the perfect comeback that comes to you long after, I was good at being a day late and far more than a few dollars short (thanks for *that* gift, great thief, Becca). My missing l'esprit de l'escalier must've been down the squeaky clean toilet I'd cleaned along with all the money she stole from us.

If you're doing a body count, that's six total friends lost to me because of business. Because I cared, probably too much, I gave an inch, they took a mile, or at least that's how it felt, and on paper, that's how it looked.

Lesson learned. Finally.

When people say never ever hire friends, they mean it. Even family would've been challenging, but blood is thicker than water. Families work through challenges, friends just say, "Fuck it, I'm out."

Right about this time, Mamabargains was named the winner in the 'Totally Awesome Awards', a voter generated contest with half a million votes. On the same day we won, our site crashed—again.

The irony.

We were also named a winner in the 'Utah Business Emerging 8' competition. Eight successful businesses were awarded the honor as leaders in our state—and Mamabargains was one of them. If only the judges could've seen behind the scenes!

Mamabargains day-to-day would've made a great reality show. The non-stop chaos, the decision-making, grief, joy, the employees—oh, those employees.

Where YUITS was concerned there'd be no awards. These guys had gone into hiding and were now almost entirely unreachable. When catastrophe struck, and the Mamabargains site was down for two full days, I called them every ten minutes.

The sons-of-bitches didn't return my calls.

Finally I received a breezy email from James, the owner of YUITS, the one we'd initially signed on with:

"Hi Jess, We're no longer available on the weekends. I'll respond on Monday, and we'll look at a resolve then."

Meanwhile, Stanford and I were barely speaking, other than to exchange cold pleasantries.

There's not a word to describe how out of control our lives had become.

After James' don't-give-a-shit email along with facing the fact that we'd allowed thousands of dollars in stolen payroll, I could think of only one way to prevent the impending disaster to my business, family, and life.

These assholes would have to pay serious consequences for their actions.

I was convinced I was dealing with deliberate sabotage. Someone, something, was trying to kill Mamabargains. It was time to take matters completely into my own hands.

No more leaning on employees to get the job done right.

No more trusting without it first being earned.

No gun, weapon or *pill* had enough power to settle this headache.

I picked up the phone and dialed.

It rang twice before the brusque man on the other end of the line answered, " FBI, this is Lead Investigator Doug Lattimer... *Speak*."

The first night we met, that crisp spring evening in early 2002, he asked if he could kiss me (those soft lips of his—delish). I'd never experienced anyone so genuine and polite. He told me his name was Stan. And making an excuse in my head for his inopportune timing, I thought, *I can't possibly date a person named Stanley*. I ended up giving him my number with no intention of answering if he actually called. I had my reasons.

Three hours after my friend and I left the bar that night, 'Stanley' called.

And I didn't answer.

He left a message.

And then, I wished I *had* taken his call, dammit!

"Hi, Jessica, this is Stanford. We met tonight and I just wanted to be sure you made it home safe and sound."

Sweet menstruating Mother of God, his name isn't Stanley at all. Stanford, I could handle. Stanley, well, that just reminded me, no offense if you're a handsome Stanley—of a short, fat, bald dude.

I left my shithole house in Washington with Jake-the-druggie-from-Hell, and was making a go of it in Utah. I'd been dating, too. A return Mormon missionary wanted to lose his virginity to me—he showed up at my apartment with a jar of peanut butter and said, "I'm ready to lose my virginity, and I want it to be with you". Then there was the redheaded drummer with a penchant for piercings, most notably, his Prince Albert.

My first two tries in the Utah dating pool were less than ideal.

I went out with a guy for two years who ended up cheating on me with some cool snowboarder chick. I was so busy working two to three jobs that I didn't have the time or the money to learn to snowboard with him. And it gave him reason enough to let his eyes wander to the hottie on the hill whose name wasn't Jessica.

I was better off without him. I was better off without any of them.

Being independent again, rolling solo was my new MO.

My roommate, Erica, dragged me out that night. Our destination was a local bar to listen to our friends and their band, Tanglewood. We knew the drummer, Travis, and since I had a bit of a crush on him (clearly I was going through a drummer stage), I felt fine being the third wheel with Erica and her man.

When Stanford and his buddy sat down next to me, I was mildly irritated. These dudes were cramping my style because I'd turned my attention from the drummer to the very attractive bartender who'd been serving me free beer for the past hour.

It was actually getting juicy when my future-soulmate decided to ruin the moment, setting up shop only inches from my freshly shaved legs. Slender pre-childbearing legs, I should add, which protruded from my super-short jean skirt, a lemon print blouse and platform sandals. Damn I looked good. Stanford wore a white long sleeve t-shirt that said 'Fish Lake' on it with khaki cargo shorts. Although I'd always wanted to visit the idyllic lake named after fish, fashion-wise, the t-shirt didn't exactly seal the deal for me.

We talked about fate and destiny moments after we met. I told Stan(ley) that, "The next relationship I'm in will be forever." Truthfully I was hoping to scare him off with brutal honestly so I could get my shaved legs back in the direction of the barman. But as we sat sipping our beers, the reality that we were jiving in a really oddly terrific way couldn't be ignored.

I felt it—that *spark*. It was wonderful, except for one *minor* geographical issue. Stan was moving to Germany.

And he was leaving in two weeks.

Halt. Screech. Come again?

Cool guy. Can't fall for him. He's leaving, not just the state, the *entire damn country*. What would be the point in pursuing *that*?

Trouble was, Stan and I really hit it off, and after his phone call to check that I'd arrived home safe, we kept in touch. We spent every day together until he left the country. It was more than just that, though. We kept in touch long after his departure. Even as thousands of miles separated us, twenty-four hours didn't pass without us writing or speaking to each other. There's something to be said for good ole' romantic snail mail.

And then...

Two months after he left, Stanford sent me a surprise. It was an open-ended ticket for me to come join him in Germany. I'd never traveled internationally other than Canada and Mexico for those Church mission trips. But, Germany?

I was torn. I loved my independent life. I didn't need a man to complete me. And I barely knew this Stanford guy.

"Jess, it's a once in a lifetime opportunity you can't pass up. You have to do this. Your job will be waiting if you come back to Utah," my boss said to me as he handed me the envelope with the ticket inside. Stan had sent flowers to my job, and with the flowers came the ticket that held my future. He'd cleared the idea past my boss, who was more than happy to oblige, a romantic himself.

I was single and flexible. It was my life. I was confident Stanford wasn't a drug dealer or rapist, and after boldly asking, I'd discovered his distaste for peanut butter in bed and penis piercings, so...there was definite potential. Plus, those lips.

A month later, I was en-route to the little town of Siegelbach, Germany, which is about four hundred miles South of Berlin. I kept my apartment with Erica, and we agreed I'd mail her rent each month, because I still wasn't sure how long I'd be in Germany.

I might decide I hate it and be back in two weeks. Maybe I'll really fall for this guy and stay a year.

I liked the notion of our relationship being as open-ended as that ticket was.

Even though Stan's job transfer was for two years, there were no guarantees with the romance—and naturally, not everyone was a fan of my choice to fly thousands of miles away to be with a guy I'd only known for two weeks in person.

"What does this man do for a living, Jessica?" Dad asked.

"Um, I don't know, dad. He says it's classified."

"Classified, my ass," said my worried dad.

"Dad, no, really. He's not allowed to share with me what he does. He's working on a military base. I'll be fine," I reassured him.

My mom was also worried, "Please don't go off to Germany and elope or something crazy like that."

And then from my overly protective youngest brother, who thought I was nuts, "You do know they don't speak English in Germany, right, Jess?"

"Well, it's a good thing I took German in school, then, Tyson. Ich spreche ein bisschen Deutsch," I replied.

And, I had my own concerns.

What the hell would I do while Stan was working?

What if I decided I didn't like him, after all?

What if *he* decided he didn't like *me*?

The trip had no scheduled return date, I could leave whenever I wanted to, right?

As I walked through security at Frankfurt International Airport, there was Fish Lake Stanford holding a bunch of flowers and immediately I knew it would all be okay. My heart was at ease at the very first sight of him.

"We have to hurry," he said, "We have a train to catch that's taking us to Paris for the weekend."

Is this guy for *real*?

Yes. Yes he was. He is.

I spent over a year traveling throughout Europe with Stanford. Our adventures spanned Germany, France, Belgium, the Netherlands, Italy, Austria, Switzerland and Spain. And we traveled together perfectly—the first sign of long-term relationship success.

I could fart in front of Stanford. I could brush my teeth with his toothbrush and we both felt comfortable taking a crap or pissing in front of each other. We'd reached the poopy pinnacle of relationship prosperity and bonded over our shared fondness for flatulence.

Fast forward a year and a half—it was time to head home to the States leaving our travels and adventures behind.

Stanford left his engineering job and Germany to help run a landscape venture his dad purchased. One of the many reasons I'd fallen for Stanford was the shared love of wanting something of our own to sink our teeth into. His dad's new company gave him just a little taste of what running the show would be like. Two years later, watching it crumble *almost* destroyed the yearning to have our own business, someday.

Stanford was born and raised in Las Vegas, so it seemed to be the logical place to buy our first home together. I worked a crappy little payroll and HR job at a staffing firm. Later, at an architectural company where Photoshop became a trade I learned and honed my skills in. I was always on the prowl for new talents I could put to good use later.

In 2003, a few days after Christmas, Stanford popped the question. My answer was a no-brainer—a beaming with joy 'Yes!' We already owned our first home, why not keep our story alive and spend the rest of our lives together? I'd fallen in love with Stan somewhere between the Hefeweizen at the bar the first night we met and waking up next to him in Germany—our stinky morning mouths right in each others faces. Besides, what better way to bond, than over bad breath and beer?

So began our forever love affair.

Two months after our marriage in late 2004, I finally had medical insurance again. I made an appointment for my peepers, teeth and a good ole vagina checkup. I hadn't been for years, and was sick of the constant painful periods.

From the day I was first visited by Aunt Flo, I was in misery. On many occasions, I was hospitalized after passing out from blood loss. The doctors put me on every painkiller they could think of. They tried birth control at a young age to mitigate it, but the pain remained the same.

My first post-marriage, finally insured visit was to the vagina doctor. The exam lasted about four minutes. The initial thirty seconds of the examination I was in tears of agony. The doctor's words were straight to the point, "You have stage four endometriosis and I need to schedule you for surgery *tomorrow*."

Reeling, I said, "What's endometriosis and can you fix it?"

"It's the disease that just keeps on giving," my doctor replied solemnly. "It's not as simple as 'fixing' it," it's more a matter of *managing* it."

After a quick lesson from the doctor, I called Stanford and told him the news. I was ecstatic—overwhelmed, but mostly nervous. I was excited for the simple fact that over the years when I was told, "you have a low tolerance to pain," I actually had a high tolerance because I was dealing with this disease that had taken over my reproductive organs. Without surgery, we didn't know how extensive the damage was. I was terrified, but at least I learned what'd been afflicting me all that time.

The next day I was wheeled in for surgery.

Before I woke up, the doctor shared the bad news from the surgery with Stanford.

"Jessica's right fallopian tube is filled with endometriosis and is non-functional. Her left ovary was partially damaged with a large cyst, which we removed. We've injected her remaining left fallopian tube with a blue dye, which we used to help determine if the tube is still open. It will also act as an aid in fertility."

According to the doctor, if we wanted to have a family, our best bet would be to spend the next two months trying. "The blue fertility dye should help your little swimmers reach their final destination, but it will only last approximately two cycles," He explained to Stanford.

We always planned to wait until my thirties to start a family, but here I was, twenty-seven—there was so much more for Stan and I to do before kids.

We wanted to travel again—without a carseat or stroller in tow.

We wanted to fuck on the kitchen table and skinny dip in our pool—without babies crying in the background.

We wanted to sleep in on Sundays—we *still* do.

Premature or not, travel or not, at least we got to fuck on the kitchen table. A lot.

Imagine just having surgery and being told that you have a 12% chance of ever conceiving—needing to go home from the hospital to get busy. Forget the fact that my vagina was recovering from being under the knife, and 12% wasn't amazing odds.

At least it wasn't 0%. And we had a lot of *hard* work ahead of us.

January came and went, and with it, my period. It lasted only a few days, and passed with no pain. *Is this what a normal period is supposed to be like?* Up until then, I had no idea periods could be anything other than agonizing and debilitating. So, I was happy with my new period, but...alas, we weren't pregnant.

We had one month left in which the dye inside my one working fallopian tube could aid in conception. We clearly needed to just try harder—and longer, more often, and on every piece of furniture in the house.

It was now February. I had no idea when I was supposed to have a period because they'd always been so intermittent and irregular. Six weeks after my last period, I wasn't even remotely worried—until I started puking my brains out.

Hyperemesis Gravidarium. In layman's terms: vomiting so much that water won't stay down. It could mean only one thing...

Hallefreakinlujah!

I was *pregnant*, but I was as sick as fuck.

Work, you piece of shit body, just *work*!

At five months along, I *finally* began to feel a bit better. Still nauseous every single day, but at least I was able to keep food down. I couldn't smell garlic without vomiting, and forget taking me to a sandwich shop. Something about the smell of fresh baked bread had my stomach turning. I ate a lot of cucumbers and raw potatoes with salt on them. I liked lemons and ate frozen grapes.

The worst part was the heat. July in Las Vegas was like living inside the hot, putrid asshole of Hell, itself.

Air-conditioned movie theaters were one of the only reprieves from the blow dryer heat outside. Even though I wasn't in much of a mood for a comedy, at least we'd found something to remedy my case of cabin fever.

On this particular afternoon, I felt unusual, and not in a funny way. I couldn't focus on what was going on up on the big screen, something didn't feel quite right, and I couldn't place why. Instead of grabbing dinner after, we went straight home. My body was screaming obscenities at me for even taking it outside—that heat wasn't doing me any favors.

Only a few hours after I fell asleep that night, I awoke to an intense feeling of being kicked—stabbed in the gut.

The pain was excruciating. My thoughts, of course, jumped to the notion that something was terribly wrong with our little guy.

It couldn't be labor. I didn't feel what I thought a contraction would feel like. I just felt a constant, horrible, ripping and throbbing coming from deep in my abdomen.

Is there blood? Where's the blood? I thought to myself as I frantically threw the blankets off and flipped on the lamp to get a better look down below.

"Stanford! Stannnforrrd!" I was hysterical now, Stanford jumping to attention like he thought the bed was on fire. "It's the baby. Something's wrong with the baby! The pain is unbearable!" I shouted, barely able to form clear sentences through the agony tearing at my insides.

As Stanford scooped me up and rushed me to the car, all I could think about was almighty karma. I writhed in pain with each bump of the car. Staring straight ahead, I faced my worst nightmare—losing this child would break me in two.

Maybe this was retribution for my decision years ago to have an abortion.

This time, I'll fight with everything I have to keep this child inside me alive.

"Agent Lattimer, I'm Jessica Singer, the CEO and Founder of a local company called Mamabargains.com. I don't know where else to turn but to the FBI."

After researching our website's symptoms for more than a year, I was certain there was something deliberately criminal going on. The only option left to me was the FBI, specifically the Cyber Crime Division.

I nervously explained the situation to the agent, finally admitting out loud what I'd been thinking the past year—YUITS were dishonest—intentionally screwing us over.

"We went from almost no crashes, to the site taking a shit every single day, sometimes *multiple times a day*. Our developers say nothing's wrong, and I know they're lying. The downtime began three months after they came on board."

"Do you trust your development team?" asked the intimidating Agent Lattimer, whose gruffiness was the perfect trait for nailing these guys to the wall.

"At one time, yes, I trusted them all, now...not even remotely."

"Is there anyone within your development organization that you can 100% trust?"

I told Agent Lattimer that there *was* someone that instantly came to mind on our development team—Gregg.

"Gregg will be your confidant, than. He'll be the one that helps you understand the development and coding side of Mamabargains so we can hopefully track down whoever or whatever is causing the problems, and *why*."

Agent Lattimer asked me more specific questions about coding and our systems, instructing me to gather all the information I could about the personnel at YUITS. Gregg would need to monitor all server logs for anything out of the ordinary. He gave me a checklist of things to look for that would spell trouble for YUITS and destruction for Mamabargains.

"Do you store credit card information?" he asked.

"No, I never felt comfortable with it. Since our site was custom built, it just never seemed like the smartest thing to do. Whatever is happening, it thankfully doesn't involve any customer data," I explained.

"Do you see any missing revenue? As in funds being siphoned away from Mamabargains?"

"No, funds aren't being stolen, the problem is the loss of orders and customers because of the intermittently faulty website. We went from reputable to rinky-dink."

When we hung up, a surge of hope overcame me. I was getting direction from the FBI's Cyber Crime Unit, and Agent Lattimer promised we'd get to the bottom of the crippling issue. It was time to unleash my own detective skills so the Bureau could help us.

Stanford, Gregg and I began our intensive digging on YUITS. Personal and business information on everyone within their team was what we'd been instructed to unearth. We dove into the job as if our lives depended on it. The life of Mamabargains certainly did.

It was patently obvious that our YUITS Project Manager, Damon, couldn't hold a torch to even my beginner coding and technical knowledge. During our weekly conference calls, I'd shake my head at the inept nonsense coming out of his mouth. Even worse, we were paying this amateur a premium professional rate for substandard service. I'm no fan of compensating stupidity with dollars.

But an incompetent like Damon didn't explain the complex technical issues. For a start, he just wasn't smart enough to be the actual cause. He was part of the team causing the plague, so we kept looking at the others who worked within YUITS.

Lead YUITS developer, Karrar seemed to be the only qualified developer on James' team. His offices were in the Middle East, but Karrar worked mostly out of Houston, Texas. On the days when we wanted to cut duffer Damon out of the conversation, Karrar would come to our rescue. It was clear he was as irritated by Damon's technical ineptitude as we were.

It appeared Karrar was on our side when he expressed concern over his boss' (James) lack of action and indifference to our obvious server issues. We didn't reveal the FBI's involvement to him, but hinted at our suspicions that YUITS had something to do with the downtime and shrinking revenue. Karrar knew we were on the hunt and didn't disagree with our concerns.

Then, of course, there was the main man James. We knew little about him. He had some technical know-how—that much was clear. Our detective work revealed that James seemed to have most of the experience he said he had. In our research, though, we discovered one little tidbit—We couldn't find any apps to back up his claim that he'd built several of them prior to taking on ours.

The Mamabargains' apps were eight months late, and counting.

Two weeks after speaking to the FBI, Gregg discovered something unusual while trenching through the logs—a setting (it was called 'keep alive') that was disabled. Mamabargains had been offline for over an hour during another one of our debilitating crashes. Gregg switched it to where it should've always been—*enabled*—and...

Suddenly the entire Mamabargains site was up and running again!

Was this goddamn setting disabled for an entire year? Maybe it's been the cause of all of the troubles. Why didn't our highly paid server development guys, YUITS, discover this?

Everyone in the office clapped. Gregg was our hero. There were hugs and smiles that had been missing for months. Gregg came to the rescue, resolving the source of our shrinking revenue and my panic-attacks, and all with the 'flip of a switch'.

Sheepishly dialing Agent Lattimer for the umpteenth time, I wondered how he'd react. *Did I really seek the help of the Federal Bureau of Investigation over a fucking on/off switch? Jesus, Jess.*

Like a butterfly effect, though, one small coding change could mean death to a website, or it could, and most often means fourteen other things break as a result.

Mid-ring, I noticed Stanford standing in the doorway, brow furrowed in disgust.

"What the hell is wrong *now*?"

"The celebration's over. The site's down again. The switch wasn't the cause. We're back to square one."

I hung up (slammed the phone down) before Agent Lattimer answered. Stepping into the main office, I stared at the huge website traffic monitor, shaking my head. At one time this monitor had hummed with activity, buzzing with thousands of people on our website all at once, shopping to their hearts content. In our darker days, we'd gotten used to seeing that big zero on the screen, and zero customers meant zero revenue. That day, it meant zero resolve.

It also meant Mamabargains was down again.

At our peak we'd installed the brag-worthy big screen in the office—because it was a buzz watching the numbers climb. Now it was just depressing, observing the catastrophe occur in real time, the low numbers, a direct correlation to the hole we were entering.

I looked around the office at the long faces of every single employee. A second ago they'd been celebrating, now, they were back in the depths of despair. All eyes were on me, the fearless leader standing in front of them. We all stared at that big depressing zero on the one hundred and three inch screen towering over us in the middle of the room.

For the first time since we'd installed it, I turned the motionless screen off. That was the only way I could think of diffusing the sadness in the room.

They were devastated, we all were. It was my duty to encourage them.

I opened my mouth to speak once, twice, three times, but no words came out.

I didn't have answers to offer. I had no speech, no inspirational magic to toss their way.

I made eye contact with every employee, looked at Stanford, and then walked back into my office, shutting the most-of-the-time-open door behind me.

I felt like dying—screaming into a pillow that wasn't even there. I wanted to throw something, to punch the wall.

I didn't want to admit to my frailties. I needed to find strength, but their crestfallen faces were more than I could bear. The disappointment felt personal, and—after the false celebration—I realized that layoffs were reality.

Someone or several someone's had to go.

I opened my drawer and popped two Zoloft.

There's a bottle of gin somewhere in here.

Where's that damn thing? Ah...there it is, right beneath the trinket that Senator Bennett of Utah gave me after I spoke at his entrepreneurial business conference.

I set the Senator's gift on my desk and stared at it, placing the gin by its side.

The burden was too heavy. To the staff, the screen meant boredom. It meant that their day wouldn't be full of customer service calls, vendors to communicate with or orders to fill. The quiet screen simply meant clocking out early and going home. Leaving the stress of their day behind until tomorrow.

To me, it meant disaster for my family, for our employees and vendors and for their families. More sleepless nights and less sanity was my fate. That zero represented death.

Just as I hit rock bottom I heard Justin Timberlake. The ring tone on my phone when the nanny or one of my kids was calling was 'Cry Me A River'. Quite fitting.

"Mom?" The little voice on the other end of the line said, "How's your day?"

I looked down at the bottle of gin and tucked it back into the drawer, still unopened—where it had been resting for over a year. I put on a brave voice for my oldest boy, Noah—His impeccable timing pulled me from the depressed stupor. "So great, buddy! Especially now that you called!"

Afterwards, cold, hard clarity came.

I pulled out a notepad and wrote every employee name down.

It was time to face the tough decisions.

Because I had a family of my own to care for—sacrifices had to be made.

What do I do? Layoff the long term and highest paid?

Lowest pay and most recently hired?

What about legal ramifications?

How about one person from customer service?

That's too valuable of a position.

It would fall on my shoulders to cover after laying them off, and I already had too much on my plate. Plus, *when* we recover, it would cost me more in training labor to rehire for that role.

Maybe one or two people from the warehouse?

Stanford and myself, along with customer service, could pick up the slack. It was the only position that didn't require much training, which made it the most viable option.

Firings I'd gotten used to, but *mass* layoffs? A whole different beast. And I didn't take the decision lightly.

Be practical, do the best thing to keep the business afloat and at least keep some staff still earning. Downsizing is no joke.

In the end, I chose to layoff three warehouse employees and cut back on all management hours. We still had revenue coming in—we'd just have to run the business thinly. I kept the bare minimum of staff to keep my head above the quickly rising waters of doom.

We cancelled the bottled water deliveries. Wouldn't want to drown.

We cut back on excess everything. No more donut Fridays.

We let our PR team go. We couldn't even afford to pay their last bill.

I stopped buying employee lunches. Especially for Hailey and Jane.

We took away the employer paid portion of Health Insurance—pre Obama-care, of course. Because as a small business owner, these are the things that you have to do when the going gets tough, and no more of that vision and dental coverage, either.

Man up and put your big girl panties on. It's business. Enough of the employee relations, bounce back over to tech issues, now.

Consider all of the possibilities. Then adapt.

This is what owning a business is all about.

If something seems too good to be true...it is.

No way the entire tech problem resulted from one small little flip of a switch.

You know better. Nothing is ever that simple.

Execute your decision without delay.

If you think too long and hard about it, you'll change your mind—do it, Jess.

What's that old saying about what goes up must come down? Or rather, what is given can later be taken away? Oh Lordy, I just half-ass quoted the Bible there, again, see that? What the Lord giveth, the Lord taketh away. In the midst of all this chaos, our past successes were catching up with us.

The next day, we received notification that I was named a finalist in the 'Ernst & Young Entrepreneurial Winning Women' contest. I didn't feel like a winner as I looked at the list of potential employees getting the axe on my notepad.

Mamabargains was honored in the 'Top 25 Women Owned Businesses' by Utah Business Magazine—the same day we laid off the first warehouse employee.

A month later, Mamabargains was named one of twenty winners in the 'Women Online, Fastest Growing Women Owned Businesses of 2013 (WO20)'. Yep. We were one of the fastest growing companies—and we were right smack in the middle of layoffs.

Hi, my name is Jessica Irony Singer.

The awards kept rolling in, demonstrating to me that Mamabargains was worth fighting for. We were renowned for doing great things, but no one really knew the pain that was going on behind closed doors. Those that suspected something was amiss believed that my reputation as the businesswoman who can *fix anything* would extend to this latest crisis.

I was engrossed in the research Agent Lattimer assigned us—obsessed with finding the 'answer'. We were attempting to put a puzzle together that still had half of its pieces missing. Even with three people—Stanford, Gregg and myself—digging through server logs looking for the smoking gun, it was like looking for a damn needle in a haystack.

Zoloft was no match for this level of anxiety.

Days turned into weeks, then months sifting through hundreds of thousands of lines of confusing code looking for anything unusual. We were running ourselves into the ground, spending countless hours looking for a hallelujah moment.

And, it looked like our diligence may have paid off.

That's odd. How'd we miss that before? And, why was the server accessed using that method of logging in? Even I knew better.

We discovered the IP address of whoever accessed our servers and disabled the 'keep alive' function only moments before the site went down that terrible day. IP addresses are unique strings of numbers that identify the location of a computer or a server. Just like the address on your house, or the license plate on your car.

The location of the invader?

Houston, Texas.

Who did we know in Houston, Texas?

None other than our seemingly friendly and always helpful programmer, Karrar.

Wait, YUITS told us they were nowhere near the servers when it went down, that they were with another client that day.

Fuming now, blood about to boil over. *Liars*!

"Agent Lattimer? I have something you'll want to see. We've found that someone accessed our servers using the root login privilege (I'll explain the meaning below). The access point was in Houston, Texas—I have the IP address verifying it. These guys, YUITS, they're liars," I explained.

And when I read him the line of code, Agent Lattimer was shocked.

"Jessica, root login is the administrator login of *all administrators*, a superuser. *No one* should be using that form of logging in, *ever*. You're telling me that YUITS—Karrar—used it? It should be disabled on your servers. *They* should've disabled it."

Not even Stanford or Gregg had root login privileges. They had their own personal logins that YUITS assigned them, so I knew that they knew better. A root login user can ~~cover~~ erase their tracks.

Apparently this was a track that YUITS had forgotten to erase.

Agent Lattimer, banishing any remaining doubts, confirmed my suspicions that the IP *did* belong to Karrar, or at least someone in his office location in Houston, Texas.

What could he expect to gain from damaging the reputation of our company? It didn't make sense. What other reason could Karrar have for accessing our servers, blatantly changing a setting, and then later vehemently denying it?

I asked Agent Lattimer point blank, "Do you believe that Karrar may be engaged in terrorism, using my company as a front for possible illegal activity?"

I was reaching.

I breathed a sigh of relief when he thought it unlikely since there was no literal revenue being stolen from Mamabargains' accounts. Agent Lattimer said cyber-terrorists are almost always after one thing—money.

One thing was certain, though, it was time to confront James. I'd had enough of their lies, and was terrified over what else we'd uncover as we persisted in our search for answers.

Put a stop to this. Now.

"James, we're losing more revenue every single day. Our customers are leaving in droves. I've laid off three employees, cut hours back on several others and have reduced overhead in every area humanly possible. Your team is responsible for this mess. What do you plan to do about it?"

"It's not my problem, we aren't renewing our contract with you, anyway. I won't take anymore of this abuse from Mamabargains," James said.

"Abuse? Are you joking? So you think it's *abusive* for us to *expect* that you do the job we are *paying* you well to do?" I replied.

So, he was telling me (with no subtlety) that he didn't want to renew. He expected me to think that he'd have our best interest in mind throughout the remainder of the contract? Bologna. I'd take this matter into my own hands. He's the one that ended the contract, but he didn't do it with those words, he *did it* with his inability to provide the services we'd paid for.

End of story. And we still didn't have our fucking apps completed. Asshole.

To: James @ YUITS

From: Jessica Singer

Subject: Urgent

James,

At the end of this rolling contract, three months from now, Mamabargains will not be renewing services provided by YUITS. You'll complete our apps, which are now eleven months late. You'll provide us each help ticket and its details that we've submitted over the past year. I *will not pay* the last month's bill—until everything I requested is complete. Further communication can be directed to our attorney.

Regards,

Jessica and Stanford Singer

We'd have to hire someone new (again), someone that specialized in the administration and security of servers. Not only that, but whoever we find would have to get up to speed and be trained on all aspects of our coding from the very people we were replacing, *YUITS*.

We'd have to delicately balance the tight-rope-walk for the remainder of our contract with YUITS. It was a risk we had to take, because replacing a development team when your company generates revenue in the six figures each year is no small feat. We didn't trust them, but we had no other option.

The FBI was willing to physically come to Mamabargains once YUITS was no longer there. They'd look at the code with the new person we found as a YUITS replacement. This was vital to our continued success, to find whatever damage was done, before it was too late, and then hopefully fix it. Agent Lattimer would be there to help us through it.

We had little information to go on, but the IP address leading us to Houston—to Karrar—was a start.

Switches, and screens, FBI Agents and conspiracies—Mamabargains terrorists, awards, layoffs, Zoloft and Gin, I was neck-deep in complications of life, of our successes.

Just roll with it, that's how I coped in the past. Why should now be any different?

Now is no different, Jess. Refuse to be a victim. Find your chick balls.

Quick, someone pin a rose on my nose - I'd finally, officially, fired YUITS.

The closest thing I could get to that rose on my nose was instead, a visit to the Saint Rose Hospital emergency room in Henderson, Nevada, uncertain of what would happen next. The pain in my abdomen was unbearable. I was hooked up to machines to monitor the baby as they attempted to find the pain source.

Shortly after I was admitted, the doctor offered news, "The baby is okay for the moment, but your white blood cell count is through the roof. It's normal when you're pregnant, but also typical of appendicitis. Combined with the nausea and vomiting symptoms, we'll need to remove your appendix."

Appendicitis? You stupid body of mine, work! I'm barely five months along!

I tried to stay calm as the surgeon explained our options.

"We can operate—though, if we disturb the uterus or cervix, there's a chance you'll go into labor. If that happens, it's likely that if baby is born, he won't survive. The other possibility is the appendix bursting if we *don't* operate, greatly increasing the risk of death to both you and the baby. I'll give you ten minutes to make the decision, Mr. and Mrs. Singer. Time is of the essence."

Considering the risks, we chose surgery. We didn't want to take the chance of the appendix bursting—and before we had time to change our minds, our ten minutes was up.

What if we lose the baby?

The nurses prepped me for surgery—racing time itself.

A cold metal table and bright lights were the next memory. The nurse saying, "She's coming-to."

The stomach pulling sensation through my anesthetized fog. I wasn't completely 'under'—deep anesthesia would've been dangerous to the baby.

I watched the hallway lights speed by—flashing—like I was in a helicopter. Stanford, nurses, *people* flew by. The hospital bed was moving—surely I was dreaming.

Am I dead?

The pain returned. I thought the surgery was supposed to fix it, but the sharp, grueling post surgery pressure was different, more central to my stomach.

After a moment, the stomach tension/wave subsided.

I opened my eyes to a huge, swelteringly hot room, buzzing with too many nurses to count.

Stan sat next to me, holding my hand—he seemed alarmed—confused.

The incessantly obnoxious beeping, and the—*fuuuuuuck!*

*What's that tightening and awful feeling rising in my stomach
again?*

I felt down below to where I'd so frequently and proudly rested my
forearms on my small, growing belly.

He's still in there.

"Stan? What's happeni...?" —another wave, taking my breath away
with its intensity.

"You're having a contraction. You're in labor," He said, sullen in
response.

"In *labor*?"

"Yes, they're trying to stop the labor. They removed the appendix,
but before they did, you went into labor on the operating table. You're in
critical care in the maternity ward."

A stern looking nurse rushed in, injected my arm with her syringe
of doom and as she turned to huff off, I asked, "What the hell's that for?"

"That's Brethine. Hopefully it'll stop the labor. You'll get one shot
every fifteen to thirty minutes until labor subsides," she explained.

The room felt like it was 180 degrees inside. I was heavily dosed
with Magnesium, which makes you feel hotter than shit. Everyone that
entered wore warm coats because the air conditioning was keeping my
dungeon as cold as the thermostat would allow. I was naked, no blankets on
my body, but sweating bullets. I was told it was 117 degrees outside—a
record high in Las Vegas that July 19th, 2005. My room felt hotter.

Hearing about the appendectomy, Mom flew in from Washington State. She'd go from pacing Satan's perspiring armpit outside—stressfully puffing away on her ~~cancer sticks~~ cigarettes—to re-entering my hell hath frozen over hospital room. I barked at the nurses who weren't only injecting me, they were starving me in case another surgery or emergency C-section was necessary. Through all of it, I was still contracting.

Three days after surgery, the around the clock injections (they'd given me more than fifty total) stopped the labor. My contractions became sporadic rather than regular.

I was sent home, the new 'baby on board' sticker on our car carrying an entirely different meaning.

I was home free, ready to finish out the last few months of my pregnancy on bed rest, and to meet my little bundle of baby. My diseased bomb shelter of a uterus actually protected the little dude inside.

I thought having an emergency appendectomy while I was pregnant was bad.

That was a picnic compared to birth. Fair warning—if you want the filtered version, stop reading or skip the rest of this chapter.

Because there's no filtered version of birth.

Don't look at the epidural needle in birth class—resist the temptation. That needle is gigantic, *long*. It goes into your back along your spinal column. Try having a contraction while a needle is being inserted *into* your *back*. The anesthesiologist tells you, "Don't move—there's a very slight, rare possibility of paralysis if you move and we hit the wrong nerve in your back."

Not that birth itself isn't pressure enough.

Once that bad boy goes in, the pain should melt away, right? Wrong!

I felt everything. Every birth is different, and we all endure pain differently. Hopefully you aren't part of my club—the one that experiences agony before, during and *after* the epidural.

If you have to *wonder* what back labor pain feels like and *if* you experienced it during birth, you *didn't* have back labor. The feeling of someone ripping your spine out from your asshole up through your mouth while simultaneously injecting your sides with straight botulism—that's back labor.

Tear that shit up.

Literally, your vagina might—will likely—rip. Like paper, but through skin—layers of skin. To episiotomy or not to episiotomy, that, my friends, is the question. You do *not* want to become one with your anal sphincter during childbirth.

I chose to let 'er rip.

Oh. My. God.

You know the worst pain ever?

Paper cuts. Paper cuts are terrible little slices of hell.

Can you see where I'm going with this?

Men, want to know what it feels like to tear as you are birthing a five to ten pound (or more) bowling ball through your vagina? (Ladies, this is your cue to hand the book to your spouse or significant other and let them continue the informational reading.)

No? Aw, come on, you're tough right?

Bullshit. No man I know would take a piece of *cardboard* to his manhood, to the head of his household down below, to his one eyed snake. Not a piece of paper, a piece of *cardboard*.

JESSICA SINGER | 195

Now, slice that shit up—just one big thick slice right across that nifty little pee hole of yours. But go deep man, horror movie shit, right? Yeah, birthing a baby is like a horror movie—guts, gore, blood, bodily fluids, and smells, all of it. Okay, now that you've sliced yourself up with a thick piece of cardboard, try pushing a *bowling ball* through that small hole. I don't care how large of a hole you have. Pushing *anything* through any of your bodily orifices is going to be painful. Don't let anyone tell you any different.

Don't forget to breathe. Hee-Heee-Hooooo. Hee-Heee-Hooooo.

That's how I coped with the torture chamber they call a 'birthing room'. I made it through, like thousands of other women who birth babies every day, living to tell the tale.

PS, A baby isn't the only thing that's going to come out—be prepared to poop, to fart and to pee, all while birthing. If you're a prude, good luck to you. It's best to let inhibition leave the room. Be secure in the fact that fourteen people or more may see your vagina.

You might be poked and prodded—hot and bothered. Not the 'screaming at your husband during birth' kind of aggravated, but the 'get your finger out of my hoo-ha for the third time in the past hour' kind of irritated. It's okay to be annoyed that the nurse has dandruff, that her breath makes you want to punch her in the face, or that her fingernails are tattered and sharp. The ridiculous beeping coming from the monitors while you try to rest for two minutes between contractions is no picnic, either. Don't forget the elasticized waist strap with the hard plastic monitor attached to it. It tightens, digging into your belly with every contraction, causing understandable agitation.

Birth isn't easy or pleasant. *No one* really looks as pretty as the image they uploaded to social media makes them appear afterwards. That's what makeup is for. It's not called labor for nothing, people.

You'll look as ragged as you feel. Well, 99% of women will, if I had to guess.

Me? I looked like death after birth—probably because I felt like death, too.

Steal ice chips. I don't care if the nurse says no liquids and that you can't eat anything. Make your husband or partner steal those frozen morsels to keep your mouth moist. But be stealthy, and don't blame me if you get caught.

Keep your lips slathered in lip moisturizer. Chapped lips are a distraction.

Bring lavender—or any other kind of pleasant essential oils—focus on that instead of Nurse Bad Breath's stinky armpits while you are deep breathing through those contractions.

After being induced a week after my due date, I endured fifty-five hours (three-thousand-three hundred minutes) of labor, with five straight hours of pushing. I had multiple doses of epidural, until they refused to offer me more. I back labor birthed the bigheaded, blonde mohawked munchkin with only Morphine for the pain. After my entire body broke out in hives, it was clear I was allergic to the last resort drug they'd given me— so I birthed the baby doped up on Benadryl. I was telling jokes and singing songs, unaware of the audience that'd gathered. At least that's the story I'm told.

The little guy came out purple with a cone shaped head from the vacuum suction they used to help get him out. I'd birthed a new breed of partially blue smurf child.

He was posterior—the back of his head against my spine and sacrum—causing the excruciating back labor I'd endured.

There's a picture of me breastfeeding my cone-headed, deeply plum colored little smurf dude for the very first time—and I have no recollection. After hearing the relief of his cry, I passed out, exhausted from the more than two days of labor. Women are apparently capable of amazing things—incoherently breastfeeding is one of them. Singing and joke telling must've worn me out.

After birth, when you use the restroom, you'll get to wear boat-sized pads. They give you one size fits all net-like underwear—huge and stretchy to hold the monstrosity of a yacht-pad in place. Best invention ever. My vagina always wanted to model cheesecloth on the runway. Don't forget the squirt bottle they give you to soak your once upon a time pink taco with warm water. Save those. They are a big hit at bath time later on for the kids at home. If they only knew they were once used as vagina squirt bottles. Shhh.

Cold pack vagina pads—also a super invention! They keep your lady parts on ice while they're throbbing with searing post-birth pain. Take a handful home too, those period pad ice packs have multiple uses and are great on your forehead for a headache down the road. They even have a sticky adhesive backing! When your husband uses one for his bum knee—please take a picture.

By the way, breastfeeding for the first time sucks too. No pun intended.

Bring a beer with you to the hospital, one that's barley rich. My milk wasn't coming in, so a few days after we brought the baby home from the hospital, we read the wives tale and I drank a beer. My milk came in with a vengeance within a few hours and I've got the picture to prove it. My boobs grew to the size of cantaloupes (originally the size of mosquito bites)—Dolly-Parton-gigantic and dripping milk from each nipple.

Bringing the little man home from the hospital, all wrapped up, snug as a bug in a rug, we were absolutely exhausted.

This parenting thing is going to be a snap.

Stanford and I looked at the baby, then at each other, then back at the baby, "Now what?" we said in unison.

A week after we brought Noah home from the hospital, Stanford was laid off from his job at his entrepreneur dad's business—the one we'd left Germany for. Seemed no better time than the present to pursue another life adventure for the Singer clan.

Stanford's old engineering employer rehired him, meaning a relocation for our little family from Las Vegas back to Salt Lake City. We figured it'd only be a matter of time until our little monster, Noah, asked what XXX spelled had we chosen to stay and raise him in Las Vegas. Plus, in-law family dramas were plentiful and we couldn't wait to get the hell out of sin city.

The stars were aligned as our Vegas house sold in under a week.

Getting the fuck out of Dodge.

A month later, we were back in Salt Lake City, Utah—the place that had brought us together more than three years before. We were rich with a happy marriage, a nice house, a healthy baby, and a good job.

But...

We wanted more.

The endometriosis wreaked havoc—again. I opted to have another laparoscopy so that my doctor could get an idea of just how bad it had again gotten. He 'cleaned it up', leaving my periods easier to manage once more. Like a car after an oil change, purring like a kitten, or an enema, (yeah, that's a good analogy, too) my body thanked me. Two months after that second surgery, and only five months of trying, we were pregnant again.

I was sick for nine months straight, preterm labor beginning only five months into the pregnancy. I was ordered to take it easy, which was kind of difficult with a toddler at home. Progesterone shots in my ass once per week to control the contractions and hopefully keep my body from going into full labor were required. Progesterone is as thick as olive oil. That shit burns going in and leaves your ass muscle seizing up for almost a week. About the time the pain goes away from one shot, it's time for the next.

Our second boy was born in Salt Lake City, two years and two months after Noah. Welcome to the world, Elijah!

With Noah and Elijah, our little agnostic family would blend into Mormon country especially well. Our little boys with biblical names would make the door-to-door evangelicals assume we already had God, so, #winning.

Eli's birth was much smoother than Noah's. I knew all the tricks of the trade, and having a badass doula on delivery day helped me immensely (thanks Hilary!).

The birth may have been uneventful, but when we got Eli home, his crying began almost immediately. At first, it was an hour at a time, then two hours. Nothing could've prepared us for the eventful first few weeks of his life. The newborn crying worsened—I couldn't figure out what was wrong with this helpless little child.

Soon, the crying went from lasting a few hours between feedings, to every single minute between feedings. The only time he wasn't screaming was when he was breastfeeding. The only time he was sleeping, was when he was eating. That meant the only time I could sleep, was when he was eating.

Friends and family would tell us it was colic. Colic? What the fuck is *colic*, anyway? It's actually something bigger than anyone wants to admit, in *my opinion*. It's your baby's way of telling you that there is something wrong. It's his way of communicating that he's uncomfortable, in pain or unhappy in some way. Listen to him. Elijah would breastfeed and two minutes later, projectile vomit—an exorcist style heave that'd fly three or four feet out of our tiny, seven-pound human.

Thank the blue skies that I listened to my gut (his gut).

It's extremely depressing to deal with non-stop crying. This is one reason why women experience postpartum depression. It's why babies get suffocated, and why baby shake syndrome exists. The amount of stress a new, sleep deprived mom endures while her baby cries non-stop with no support system in place is no laughing matter.

Noah said, "Make it stop, mommy. Make Eli stop crying!"

There was no one in state to help us.

I just need a break. Someone, anyone, help!

You'll feel alone, but you aren't. Your husband or partner has gone back to work already and they get to clock into normalcy every day, leaving behind the chaos that you're left with. At least I wasn't a single mom—props to you, if you are.

You might feel bitter. Please don't. It's a brief moment in a huge chunk of time.

I'd read it in all the pamphlets and laughed. What mom would ever *harm* her child? Thank goodness I'm bull-headed and stubborn. I refused to allow the stress to sink me—the brief thoughts of smothering him were tormenting enough.

"Stanford, you've got to come home right now. I can't make him stop crying. I'm exhausted. I can't listen to it anymore. I'm losing my mind."

I hadn't slept for more than three hours in two-days. And I was trying to care for our toddler with a screaming baby on my hip.

We insisted that the doctor do tests on Elijah because my total elimination diet for thirty days did nothing to help him. I thought he was getting something that didn't agree with his belly through my milk, but I was wrong. They did a full blood work panel along with stool samples. We waited, while listening to our constantly crying 'colicky' baby.

No one offered to come and hold him for an hour so I could get some rest.

All I had were people, *family,* offering unsolicited (and unhelpful) advice.

Baby massage wouldn't help him—this was more than just sore muscles.

Baby chiropractic? Nope, no thanks.

Acupuncture for my few week old little one? No way!

Feeding him homemade formula? Not a chance!

It hardly seemed like the time to use my child as a guinea pig, experimenting on him like a lab rat. The recommendations from every direction were more depressing than our non-stop crying baby, adding to my list of new mom hardships.

My advice: Don't offer a new mom advice!

Offer to hug her, to hold the baby—let her catch a few hours of precious sleep if you *really* want to help. Make *her* lunch, or dinner. Bring her flowers.

The tests came back,

"Stop breast feeding immediately. Elijah is showing signs of being allergic or highly sensitive to your breast milk. Not just *your* breast milk, but breast milk in general!" His little tummy isn't digesting or metabolizing the sugar galactose, which is naturally found in breast milk. His intestines are filled with a build-up of bacteria from the undigested galactose."

My breast milk could've killed him—the poor little guy was so sick. Elijah was fed a hypoallergenic formula from that day on, thriving wonderfully from his first bottle. The vomit after feedings and mucousy bloody stools disappeared. Thankfully moms are armed with 'motherly instincts'. Mine told me that 'colic' wasn't the answer. I was right to listen to *my gut.*

And I didn't get any high fives from the previous suggestion-givers.

Instead, the ones whose instructions I'd disagreed with in favor of my own instinct, I inadvertently created bad relationships with that followed me forever. How *dare* I disagree.

I was a stressed as fuck, sleep-deprived mom just wanting the best for my child.

Persist to find the answer to the problem and don't stop until you figure it out. Nine times out of ten, baby is just being fussy, but that one time in ten—that's what you've got to watch for. This little man was the one in ten, and time wasn't on his side.

Some day, I'll be able to tell Eli that no matter how much he wants to try it, when his wife has a baby and her boobies are filled with milk— resist the temptation, man!

Noah, my comic relief helped keep me sane. At the age of two, he was keeping me on my toes, and he definitely had no filter—like mother like son. With a smiley baby on the mend and a nutty busybody toddler on my hip, I found joy in the ordinary again—like a simple visit to the grocery store.

I needed a fresh stock of all things feminine hygiene—lady absorbables. Pads with and without wings, panty liners, regular, super, extra super, extra long tampons—right next to those, the adult diapers.

Why can't that old guy just hurry up? This is my aisle, man. I was here first!

Noah was a good talker and walker already, and I spoke to him as I would with an adult—none of that googoo gaga shit was allowed in our home.

Well, this is fun. Why don't we just all hang out in this aisle together, perusing adult diapers and fire crotch stuffers.

Noah, observant of the world around him and well aware of what I was doing in the aisle—because a mom gets no privacy—shared what was on his mind.

The clever little shit proclaimed, in his most defined, loud, toddler English, "Mommy need *buh-guy-nuh* bandaids?"

Vagina Bandaids?

That's fucking clever.

Perhaps it was the universe's way of breaking a smile on old guy's face, because I could see in my peripheral that he found the comment equally as amusing as I had.

That was the moment I realized everything was going to be okay.

We had a home in Salt Lake City and were building our lives. Stanford's job was great and I was two years into being a stay-at-home mom.

From the day I was old enough to have a job, and even before that, I'd worked. I loved staying busy and being social, but despite all the work two boys entailed, I was really starting to miss a traditional work place.

I'm really not sure I'm cut out for this whole stay-at-home mom thing.

I needed more than the small design business I'd started after Noah was born.

I wanted more than spit up, boogers and shit-filled diapers.

Because two kids under age two weren't keeping me busy enough!

The passing thought became obsession.

What defines me? My marriage and kids?

What's my passion? Family or work?

Can't I have both?

"It's done. YUITS is done."

There was silence for a few seconds while Agent Lattimer digested my words:

"That's great news, Jessica. Let me know when you have a replacement hired and up to speed so we can determine the extent of damage and next best steps."

We still had to find a reliable, trustworthy replacement for YUITS. Perhaps the biggest issue was that YUITS still had three months left on their contract *and* they'd be involved in the hand-off to our new person. Because of their blatant dishonesty, I needed to get security steps in place to track their every move. I was hell bent on resurrecting Mamabargains and getting sales back to our hey-day levels ASAP.

Keep your enemies close...

Whenever there was a technical problem, we submitted it to what YUITS called their 'help desk ticket system'. It tracked the full detail of any reports related to site troubles, along with how YUITS resolved (or rarely did) the issue.

It was astonishing to read the cold-hard numbers: there were 516 total help desk tickets from the eighteen months YUITS was with Mamabargains. Of those, 502 of them remained *unresolved*. More compelling, YUITS failed to fix 97% of the jobs they were contracted and paid to resolve.

I downloaded each help ticket from their system for myself, screen-shotting my work along the way—in case I needed it later.

The details I compiled were mostly to benefit the new tech person. Tracking exactly what YUITS had been up to from day one would give the new hire a baseline and lateral timeline. It was a stupendous feat—adding an extra one hundred plus hours on top of my usual sixteen-hour days.

I'm already invisible mom and wife, what's more hours away from home really going to do at this point? Screw up my marriage (more), piss my kids off (more), or give me (more) anxiety? All of the above? Probably.

While we paid the YUITS deadbeats, we realized we weren't alone in making massive sacrifices. The impact reached further than we expected. Gregg had stopped billing us. He saw the financial distress we were in—everyone could. Gregg was working for us full time as an independent contractor, giving us his time *for free*. He cared for our company, for what we stood for, and for Stanford and I.

Do you know how hard it is to ask for help when you need it most? Almost impossible.

I wished I could've given him the money I was paying YUITS.

After an arduous search, we found the perfect fit to replace the YUIDIOTS. Since we'd reduced in size to such an extent, we couldn't afford a whole tech team. Lone wolf Ben possessed a background in the security administration of servers. Perfect.

We knew Ben could help solve the crippling mystery of what exactly was causing the annihilation of Mamabargains. He pumped air into my collapsing lungs, allowing me to breathe again. Even so, the tremendous amount of pressure we put on him from day one left me wondering if my confidence in him would result in a diabolical mix of his ego and my expectations, ending in our ruination.

Ben was a fast learner and a hard-worker, adding to our great team—Gregg and Ben were the new heart of Mamabargains.

YUITS' last weeks were unbelievably stressful. Talk about walking on eggshells! Keeping a professional rapport with them through to the end was one of the hardest things I've ever had to do.

Apart from the fact I wanted to throttle them for throttling us, I was terrified of what this bunch of incompetent jackasses would do to Mamabargains before their time was up. The antagonistic relationship unsurprisingly didn't end well

Everything we'd asked of them, they faulted on.

We requested all of the tickets—even though I'd already copied them from their system myself. I wanted to see what they'd provide. I pivoted my passion into catching them in their lies. And I was more than good at it.

YUITS provided a list with just *five* tickets to Ben—five out of the 516 total. Naturally they tried hiding the fact that the other 97% of the tickets were incomplete.

The most frustrating part was that we'd caught them cheating and lying so many times throughout the contract, but still couldn't figure out why. Apart from the obvious, what was in it for them to be slowly throttling our company? Even the dumbest of parasites knows you must keep your host alive to survive, just ask any tapeworm.

And then there were the outstanding apps, *still*. An infuriating twelve months late, our demands that the damn things be completed fell on deaf ears. We also requested YUITS wrap up all open tickets *finishing* their work on each of them so that we had full closure rather than being left with a bunch of open-ended inadequacies.

I'm an optimist.

However...

They finished nothing.

Nada.

Zilch.

They completed zero (0) open tasks.

Our Android and Apple apps that cost us thousands and thousands of dollars never saw the light of day during the YUITS malicious occupation of Mamabargains.

We'd welcomed them to our team with a big sushi lunch in the beginning. Maybe now we could consider offering them the Jessica special—gasoline sake and week old, rancid salmon. They'd never know the difference. Rotten is as rotten does.

Fuckers.

Ben and Gregg created a full backup of *everything*, just in case these shit-for-brains decided to wipe Mamabargains off the face of the planet in one dastardly apocalyptic final deed. The delete button did that—instilled terror.

I was looking forward to YUITS' final day like a kid does Christmas. September 22nd, 2013 was marked on every calendar in the office, the countdown on. Our entire staff was anxiously ready to celebrate a YUITS-free existence. This was as big of a celebration as our Procter and Gamble partnership celebration. Possibly bigger.

We stayed up until 11:59pm the night before the contract was officially over so that precisely at midnight, we could lock them all out forever. Ben and Gregg were prepared to batten down the hatches and flush YUITS down the toilet, closing the door on them for good. Even with the YUITS contract over, I waited for the unknown, thinking they'd come storming into the office at any moment, taking hostages for their seemingly terrorist-like activities.

Instead, the snakes slinked off into the sewer they'd crawled out of in the first place. I hope they're still there.

Ben knew exactly what he was looking for and where to search. Once YUITS were gone, the investigation was underway.

We appointed a new, short-term guy to finish the apps—and he did it in *three weeks*. It was great to have them completed, but it made my blood boil how YUITS had dragged their feet for more than a year, destroying our chance to stay ahead of the competition. Jeff Bezos, Amazon CEO says, "In business, what's 'dangerous' is not to evolve." Evolution or death.

It felt like we turned a corner. The optimism that followed took me by surprise, even though in reality our sales were still dwindling.

Ben continued his hunt for coding failures, glitches, and system weaknesses.

It wasn't long before he asked for an urgent meeting.

It was worse than any of us could've imagined.

"Every rock I turn over, there's a new issue," Ben said.

Stanford and I held our breath, waiting the worse-than-what-he'd-just-said news.

"Our firewall, the site's first line of defense, isn't configured. *Any* developer knows that a retail website of your size should have a firewall protecting its intangible assets, database and customer information, as well as the code that created the website itself."

The usually composed Ben was visibly shaken, "So much of this is *blowing my mind*. The network configuration is basically non-existent. Mamabargains runs a high traffic webserver and it doesn't even have *basic* best practices in place. The server load balancer is configured so badly, it's worse than having no load balancer there at all."

What the fuck does all of that mean, anyway? Besides the obvious—the casualties at YUITS' hands were too numerous to count.

A load balancer is like a teeter-totter. It distributes the traffic properly so that it remains leveled out, not spiking up or down. It helps when there are surges in visitors to the site, keeping it from crashing, and vice-versa.

"Why am I not surprised?" said Stanford, noticeably disgusted.

I shook my head. We were both light years away from shocked. The gravity of the situation was no stranger to either of us. But I was struggling with the implications of the firewall problem—I just couldn't grasp how any professional developer would have made such a blatant error...

Unless...

Well, unless of course, the mistake they were making wasn't a mistake at all.

Adapt or pivot. You can either turn the corner, continuing to put one foot in front of the other, or switch gears entirely.

As the next few weeks dragged by, more horrific discoveries were made. So many, in fact, that if I were to list the ways YUITS fucked Mamabargains, I'd need a separate book and another lifetime to write the damn thing.

I'm tired. Just so damn tired.

These assassins did nothing in consideration of our high traffic. Their mistakes caused traffic dips. Not a single thing they were doing was *best practice*.

The contract we'd signed with YUITS in black and white showed they were to provide DBA services—*Database Administration* services—for the administration of our servers. That's like hiring a babysitter for several thousand bucks an hour to watch your kids and she instead lets them play in the middle of a busy street dodging cars like Frogger, while she eats bonbons and watches soap operas.

In Ben's words (don't mind the tech mumbo jumbo, I'll translate in a moment): "You're paying for eight servers to run High Availability and Development, but only three are actually running. All are running single threaded with no proxies, no DNS, no NTP, and running at truncated speeds through a SPOF single port 1GB network, not 10GB, *which is absurd nowadays*."

In normal, everyday human speak, it'd be like driving on a four-lane freeway with traffic running both directions. You see an exit ahead, it says 'Mamabargains' and *everyone on the freeway* wants to go there. The freeway goes down to one lane of traffic, with no directional or stop signs, and no one is around to help direct traffic. The result? A massive traffic jam, and unless you wait an asinine amount of time, you aren't getting off on our exit any time in the next lifetime. So basically, our freeway (our network) was worthless—unless you had a tent and were ready to camp.

"Jess, it's bad. It's really bad. I don't know how to say this any other way, so I'll just tell you bluntly. We've been screwed in the dick hole by YUITS. You paid for services they never provided. You paid scam artists to run your servers. They were *not* managing those servers, Jess, and they were slowly destroying Mamabargains in the process."

"Are you certain? I know they were douchebags, we all assumed they were up to was no good, but this? It's not only negligent, it's fucking *sabotage*," I said.

We'd been riding the storm that caused our world to collapse over the previous year, and subsequently, my anger took the front seat on that road trip leading us into hell. I always thought I'd feel relief when we found the cause of all our strife, but this instead was only the aftermath of the YUITS tornado.

It'd been six months since Ben started, and we all agreed that putting a temporary bandage on these website problems would only make the situation worse.

We'd need permanent solutions.

And solutions take time *and* money.

I was reeling daily from the news Ben gave us that day in late December 2013, especially when he said there'd be more to come.

I just wanted peace. An evening with my smiling kids and husband. Family could heal me.

At home in my bedroom, I spied the dark circles under my eyes. I reminded myself of Crystal the stripper from back in the day—except without the missing rotted out teeth. And my boobs sagged—nowhere near the perky pasty laden tits I'd adorned so long ago. My skin was dull. I was haggard and exhausted. It was sad to admit it to myself, but I looked like *shit*. I'd also forgotten all about my OBGYN appointment that week. I'd gotten good at failing to take care of myself. I was just too busy to think about me.

Zoloft wasn't doing the trick anymore, so I stopped taking it. My edge was stronger than the medicine prescribed to curb its effects.

Feeling guilty about missing that OBGYN appointment I gave myself a quick breast exam.

And there it was.

What the *fuck* is that?

It kind of hurts when I touch it.

It's on the left side. It's an oval shaped lump.

Standing in the mirror now, I can see it. It's obvious enough to see it without my bra on. I'm not sure how I'd missed it, or how long it had been there...

My little breast friend, I called it.

That was me, haggard lumpy lady. I'd ridden Mamabargains of YUITS and now there was another freeloading killjoy hitching a ride on my mini melons.

Do you think I was scared?

No. I simply had to switch gears because I didn't have a choice. It was essential to take care of this unwelcome raisin resident. What we'd been going through with business, what my teen years were made of—life's little curveballs had hardened me to the reality we were facing. No matter how bad things were getting, we were still good people and because of that, we believed good karma would come our way. We had to.

After everything else, was I going to get cancer for Mother's Day?

I've always been of the mindset that if I were in a plane crash, I'd survive—I'm a fucking fighter who can get through anything. Fuck you, breast friend. Be gone with you.

Ben's 'there's more' is going to have to wait.

A day after finding the lump, showing doc and being sent to a breast specialist for a mammogram, lumpy lady was scheduled for surgery. My breast friend was 'suspect' and needed to be removed right away. I wasn't a stranger to going under the knife, and since my stripping days were long over, a boob scar wouldn't be cause for concern either.

An odd fibrous mass with a more official medical sounding name was removed by lumpectomy. All I had to do was wait for the biopsy results.

The situation at Mamabargains couldn't wait. A few hours after surgery, looped up on pain meds that made Zoloft seem like ice cream on a cold day, I was back at my desk with Stanford on speakerphone, and Ben going through the latest YUITS transgressions.

"We've learned that the database server's backup was being saved to...get this—*the database server, itself,*" Ben explained.

"What? That's like storing the backup to a CD *on the CD that you're backing up.* Even an idiot would know better—fucking dumbasses!" I said.

"Exactly. It also appears six years of Mamabargains server logs were *deleted*, they're non-existent, Jess. It's obvious that whatever they were doing, or you were paying for them to *do* that they *weren't* doing, they *intentionally* removed the history before I came on board. Only the activity related to the work Gregg and I have done *since their departure* remains. Jess, no server person in their right mind would *ever* delete those logs. There'd be no reason to unless something were being covered up."

I didn't even need to see Stanford's face at that moment, because the long-winded, frustrated sigh that we heard over speakerphone was enough to know—he was exhausted.

And there was more from Ben. Much more.

"The biggest piece of evidence I've uncovered? It would appear that as a result of your firewall never having been *configured*, someone, or a group of people—probably unrelated to Mamabargains—has been in your servers. They didn't even need to hack in to gain access. It's like Fort Knox left all of its doors and windows wide open. Be grateful that you never felt confident about storing credit card information, because there was nothing these 'hackers' took from you or your customers—other than crucial server space your customers needed to successfully process an order or even peruse your website."

"What. The. Actual. Fuck. Are you sure?"

" I'm certain. Jess, Stan, I'm *so* sorry." Ben offered his condolences, as if he was standing at the foot of our casket at the Mamabargains funeral.

That was the last puzzle piece that'd been missing for over a year.

All those times customers couldn't access our site? The endless site crashes? It was because a bunch of shitheads didn't configure our firewall. We suspected a bunch of scammers or 'hackers' may have utilized our database space to send out millions of spammy junk emails, not to our customers, but to their own lists. I wonder if YUITS were double dipping— subletting our servers and getting paid to allow a bunch of scam artists' to access them?

One wrong keystroke within our servers that the 'hackers' had full access to, and six years of code building could be destroyed. Firewalls serve a purpose, and ours wasn't set up to prevent scenarios like this from happening.

It was time to report our findings to the Feds.

When we told Agent Lattimer from the FBI, he came straight into the office to meet with Ben.

I'd spoken to this man on the phone many times before this rainy day, April 14th, 2014. We'd spent several months through Ben and Gregg's discoveries attempting to market Mamabargains—trying to win back the thousands of customers we'd lost during the time YUITS was in control of our servers, all the while discovering more and more problems.

Lattimer looked gruffer in person than he'd ever sounded on the phone. He was FBI Agent material, through and through. I was nervous to talk to him in person, fired up inside, the epitome of anger and frustration from the past year about to erupt from deep down.

Even in his casual button up shirt and slacks, he somehow seemed—intimidating, ominous.

"Glad to be here." His words left no trace of tough guy FBI agent to be found.

Shit, there was a little bit of pity in that abrupt four word sentence. Pity is never a good thing.

"Hi, Agent Lattimer, Ben has some things to show you. We're hoping you can help us with a resolve to the discoveries we've made over the past several months now," I explained, walking him over to Ben's workspace.

"I'll do my best to help you sort through it, Jess," Lattimer said.

My instinct to show him around the office and warehouse, pointing out our awards wall and introducing him to staff like I did with every other office newcomer, was muddied by the deteriorating situation we were faced with. This hardly seemed like the time to be bragging about our " knack for winning business growth awards.

Ben and the Agent sat huddled together for five nerve-racking hours.

I stayed in the quiet of my office with my nose buried in hundreds of new emails.

There was always something to do, someone to respond to. They were a welcome distraction.

Every time I found an excuse to walk past, I saw Ben explaining the litany of crimes to the stony-faced FBI agent.

I still couldn't get a handle on our situation from his expression.

I knew everything I'd poured myself into for three years was on the line and that this FBI agent would tell me straight if there was a way forward for Mamabargains.

Finally the emotionless Agent Lattimer finished with Ben, "You have a few options here, Jess," he said as he quietly closed my office door. "I think you should call your husband so he can hear what I have to say as well."

I felt that what he was about to tell me might not be the answer I'd been hoping for.

Agent Lattimer glanced over at the gold statue that always sat on my desk. The Stevie Award we'd won back in 2010 for being the fastest growing Woman Owned Company in the nation. He brushed his fingers across the engraved plate on it, finally made solid eye contact with me.

This is the moment we've waited for. He's going to help us nail these bastards. We're going to claw our way out of this with the FBI's help. Hopefully the FBI will water-board the sons-of-bitches.

As we discussed his findings, a call came in from my OBGYN's office.

Shit, the biopsy results.

I felt guilty obsessing over my personal problems—the call would just have to wait—the cancer that was destroying Mamabargains took priority over a possible personal health crisis.

After he finished, Stanford and I needed to get away to process the Agents advice.

For the first time in over a year, we got the hell out of Salt Lake City. The camping trip wasn't just R&R, it was an opportunity to reconnect and surround ourselves with love as we grappled with our biggest decision since we'd launched Mamabargains.

In the desert sands of Central Utah, we sat from sunrise to sunset, watching our kids get muddy as they laughed and splashed, building sandcastles and catching frogs. We sipped beer, holding hands, looking for the energy to deal with what needed to be done.

We smiled. We laughed. It reminded us of what life before Mamabargains was like.

At night, only the sounds of the gentle lake waves splashing along the shoreline were there to keep our family company.

I think I considered never going 'home'. I forgot where home really was over the years of business ownership. I rediscovered that home was there, by the lake with our kids and each other. It didn't matter that our sleeping bags were filled with sand and that I'd forgotten to pack clean underwear in our mad dash to get out of town. I didn't care that we had nowhere to shower or that there were stinky cows in the pasture across the way.

What mattered the most was this moment of clarity as we watched the sunset on Saturday night over Sand Hollow Reservoir. We knew that in the morning, we'd be tearing the tent down, packing up and heading back to face reality in Salt Lake City.

Entering cell service area again, my phone notifications buzzed out of control with work issues, including one from Ben wanting to know if we'd reached our decision about the future of Mamabargains. He'd been the only one in the office that knew what our weekend family getaway was really all about. There was another message to call my OBGYN...but it would have to wait.

I needed to deal with my other pressing health concern.

"The damage is extensive, Jess," FBI agent Lattimer had explained 48 hours before in the office, "In my opinion, you have two options:

"Scrap *all* of your code and start from scratch, rebuilding the entire website from the ground up, downsizing the entire business completely in the process."

"Or? You said there were two options," I asked, already knowing what the second choice was.

"I'm sorry," he replied, like a doctor delivering terminal news to a sick patient. "The other option is to close Mamabargains down."

Big tough Agent Lattimer genuinely looked like he shared my pain and wanted to give me a hug. But he couldn't because I wasn't there to receive any sympathy. I walked away before the tears began to flow, abandoning the office and leaving Stanford on speakerphone to finish the discussion.

No discussion was needed, though.

I needed to find a private place to deal with the overwhelming emotions I was experiencing. The trouble was, no such place existed at the Mamabargains. Everywhere I turned, there were faces I owed an explanation to. The staff knew the FBI Agent was coming to meet with us that day. They were excited at the possibility of a resolution to our pain. No one would've expected this outcome, a diagnosis so honest and final that it would change each of his or her lives.

Taking a quick pee break on our drive back up to Salt Lake City, I finally faced my other crisis...And the news was better. My biopsy was clean. My breast friend was gone and benign. Good karma comes to good people.

I hugged Stanford. He was as happy as I was about his once upon a time perky pre-kid fun bags, later milk mammaries only, and finally, newly rediscovered lump-free breasticles.

In that moment, as I made eye contact with my life partner, Stanford, words were unnecessary—our hearts were on the same page. Those words "for richer, for poorer, in sickness and in health, until death do we part" came to mind, because Stan and I had been to utopia and back together and we knew we could face anything thrown at us.

We were still two hours from home...And we needed gas.

Our bank account was nearing negative status—again. The credit cards were all maxed out.

The $16 in our checking account would have to work. It would have to get us through the week.

We'd drained ourselves of literally every penny we had to our name, plus some.

When Mamabargains needed transfusions we'd always been there to donate our blood. After the YUITS vampires finished feeding on us, the Singer blood bank was left overdrawn.

And we knew the best way to kill a vampire was exposure to direct sunlight. It looked like now was going to be as good a time as any for us to open the YUITS casket in broad daylight, putting their crimes on full display for the world to see.

If this were one of those Choose Your Own Adventure books, I'd refer you to the earlier chapter titled 'Dreams Do Come True'.

We had a second son, I dreamed of starting the business, and then we made it reality.

The business grew, offering us security, and our boys grew, giving us laughter.

Our bigger family moved into a bigger home. Life with a preschooler, a toddler and a 24/7 business was nothing short of spectacularly busy.

Then—oops.

In 2010, Super Sperm Stanford knocked me up, again.

Really?

Apparently our reproducing eggs and sperm used my only functional fallopian tube as a passageway to their final destination, Chateau d'eau Uterus.

The tango his little swimmers danced blew that whole claim the doctor made years before—that we only had a 12% chance of conceiving— right the fuck out of the water.

This was our last chance, unplanned, to have a daughter. I fantasized about pedicures, shopping and braiding her hair a million different ways. Tomboy Jess wanted a girl to dote upon.

We found out four months in, though, that our little girl was another little boy.

And I was devastated (sorry, Finley!)

Girls can be assholes, anyway. I've always gotten along better with the opposite sex. Plus, boys spoil their moms, so #momwin.

By twenty weeks along, I was in preterm labor again. Second time's a charm, right?

Contractions didn't stop from four months through to the very end. I was on those damn thick-as-olive-oil ass-shots every single week again like I was with Eli's pregnancy.

That year (2010) marked the first time I was interviewed on the local news station for Mamabargains' many successes.

It was announced in early 2011 by Utah Business Magazine that I was one of the 'Emerging 8' Winners. The honorees were chosen for shooting off fireworks of business success in Utah. I accepted the award practically rolling up to the stage, a ripe and round eight months pregnant. Eight must've been my lucky number that year.

For lack of a better phrase, we were rockin' and rollin'.

In Spring 2011, I went into labor. I delivered sans intervention or medication, a healthy three and a half weeks early baby boy. Eleven minutes of uneventful, natural labor. And I'd even gone to work that day. I wanted to get a full seven hours of Mamabargains work in before my scheduled weekly checkup. By the time I arrived, I was dilated to a six— nearly ready to push.

Dedication to our business always came before personal needs—even birth.

Finley's smiles lit up our world, all three of our boys' smiles did (do). We had a full time nanny, three healthy boys, and our three-year-old business was booming.

We had everything we'd ever dreamed of and more.

The Mamabargains tagline was 'Are YOU Hooked Yet?' And it was true—I was hooked.

The first drug I'd ever become addicted to. I was hooked on working, on the high that successful businesses give you. I even brought my newborn to work with me everyday, grinding hours out between feedings and diaper changes.

Mamabargains seemed better for it.

My employee, Becca, was such a great asset to the company. She was running the show while I was out for a few hours birthing a child, proving to me her worth as a leader.

Maybe I'll let her start training the new hires, Hailey and Jane.

I knew I could trust Becca, it was clear she always had our best interest in mind.

She deserves a raise, too, for her dedication.

What a catch! (That's your queue to revisit the Chapter titled 'Calling in the Big Dogs').

I wondered to myself every morning how long the dream would last.

What the hell is that tightening in my neck and what's happening in my arm?

I didn't know what was happening, but soon, the minor rotator cuff tear I'd experienced two years prior in my shoulder was returning. This time, it came back with a vengeance as it sent shooting pain down my arm and across my neck.

Maybe I'll just take a nap. I should probably just go home.

Mamabargains was every single day high-energy. Maybe I'd pushed it too much in the overworked CEO department?

And then, as fast as the labor with my last little guy happened, I found myself vomiting. Before I could scream for help, the millions of little orange-haired troll-demons inside my left arm began sawing away at its nerve endings. I thought it was on fire—the shooting pangs racing from shoulder to fingertips. The neck pain increased until it immobilized my head entirely—it's sheer weight upon my spinal column was nauseating. Within seconds, two of my fingers on my left hand were numb.

There is no way to explain the impact of neuropathy on a person's body. I don't wish it upon my worst enemy.

I screamed for help.

Stanford rushed me to the ER, because we thought I was possibly having a heart attack. One MRI later revealed I had two bulging disc herniations in my neck, in the C4/C5 and C6/C7 vertebrae.

My obsession with desk and computer work was the likely culprit.

Imagine a peanut butter and jelly sandwich. Now fill it with oozing raspberry jam. If you squash the two layers of bread together, what happens to the jam? It oozes out, right? Well, now picture each vertebra as a piece of bread. Envision the 'discs' are the jelly. My vertebrae were compacting against the discs, causing them to swell. The bulges themselves were pushing up against my spinal cord in two places, causing the intense suffering I was experiencing.

Our bodies are marvelous things of wonder, aren't they just?

Fuck that noise.

This was like nothing I've ever experienced in my life. I mean, I *tore* my vagina in three separate births, anywhere between nine and eleven stitches to fix lil' miss taint (look it up if you don't know—you're welcome).

Give me a hacksaw, please!

Is this what aging was all about?

I was bedridden for two months.

Unable to move my left arm, excruciating non-stop agony, the medications didn't touch the intensity. I'd rather have been birthing twelve babies—simultaneously.

It was the invisible injury, the type where people look at you with apprehension. They don't understand. How could they? Put me in a cast, rip my arm off, anything that would be a physical demonstration of what I felt inside—a bulging cervical herniation is nothing to fuck around with.

I wanted to *die*.

I very seriously considered sawing my own arm off.

I actually begged Stanford to chop it off at the shoulder.

It's probably a good thing I was bedridden, because if I'd been able to get my working hand on a knife...

The spinal doctor wanted to try a procedure called an Epidural Steroid Injection.

Out of sheer desperation, I agreed.

Anything that reduced or could help to eliminate the intensity, I was on board with. Because I was really tired of working non-stop on my iPad while I lay in bed with a heating pad wrapped around my left arm 24/7. This was how I'd lived for two months, popping a concoction of, at one point, eleven pills in one sitting. There were the anti-nausea, narcotics, analgesics, anesthetics, anti-seizure, anti-anxiety, and anti-inflammatories— all being pumped into my sickened body.

A spinal epidural is my only choice?

I'd said before not to look at an epidural needle in birthing class, and there's a good reason why, because I had one sticking seven inches out of my neck, staring at me like a venomous snake ready to strike. This took my already ten on the Richter scale of agony to about a twenty in four seconds flat.

"Now I'm going to inject the steroid," good ole spinal doc walked me through every step of the procedure. What a nice guy.

I screamed out loud, probably scaring off half the patients in the waiting room—the sound even shocked *me*.

But then, a miracle...

"The nerve troll is *gone*!" I couldn't believe it! The injection was well worth the payoff.

"Well, there's good *and* bad news. The procedure was successful, and you're pain-free. But, it's only *temporary*," Doc McSpine Fixer explained.

"How short is *temporary*, exactly?" I asked.

"Forty-Five minutes, at most," He replied.

"Shit. Fuck. Stanford, lets go get dinner, quick."

It'd been over a month since I'd been anywhere except doctors' appointments, MRI's, Physical Therapy strength tests, prescription refills and stupid short term fixes like the epidural steroid injection.

We headed to a little café so I could eat like a normal human being. Time was ticking on this neck-fix and I needed to make the most of the precious fleeting minutes I had left. It was like we were counting down to the last meal before death by lethal injection.

And just as we walked in, a call from the office stopped me in my celebratory tracks. One of my employees hadn't showed for her shift. The front desk customer service girl was MIA.

And vendors needed to be paid.

New sales needed approvals.

It's review time, damn it! I've got seventeen employee performance reviews I need to get written. They'll also all be expecting a yearly raise, because we'd stupidly set those standards high in the beginning by offering wage increases every single year, sometimes even more frequently.

Too bad I wasn't a regularly paid Mamabargains employee myself.

I spent more than half of my forty-five minute furlough on the phone putting out office fires, rather than enjoying a few moments of pain-freedom.

The doctor was right. Just as we'd finished our meal, the no-stranger-to-me nerve dysfunction returned. I was prepared with my portable hot pack ready in the car along with a freshly filled prescription of Oxyconton. Popping a pill, a few moments later, I slipped back into the drowsy reality of my half-there mental state.

And then I returned to the bed that was my universe for two solid months.

This was no fucking vacation. Our youngest was only a year old. I'd already missed his first birthday because of the injury.

We had a winning team between Becca, Hailey and Jane running the Mamabargains' show for me, but I wondered what our employees were thinking of me when we spoke on the phone or they received my high-as-a-kite emails?

I was so thankful for our nanny, Jenna who'd been with us about four years. She was nannying the boys and nursing me—bringing me meals and medication as I lay on my king bed jail cell, chained by a hotpad and pills.

Even though I was in a hurry to get better so that I could fully focus again on Mamabargains, my efforts were to no avail. Physical therapy and meds were doing nothing. The injection short-lived. After a few more weeks in bed, my doctor decided something radical was needed.

"You have no range of motion or strength left in your left arm, Jessica. Your muscles have degenerated to the point that the damage may now be permanent. The medications aren't working. We should consider scheduling you for a spinal fusion surgery immediately."

The spine doctor explained to Stanford and I what exactly the process would entail.

"It's a major surgery, and at this point, it's all I can recommend to get your life back."

There'd be a metal plate in my neck forever, and I'd feel like I had a sore neck every day for the rest of my life, but anything was better than what I was going through.

Surgery was scheduled, and I was desperately looking forward to being well again.

Until my trusty ole gut nudged me again.

And we all know how important it is to listen to your gut.

Being operated on wasn't much cause for concern, since I was a pro, but an uneasy feeling plagued me.

I was scheduled for a Monday. And on the Thursday before, I stopped taking all of the medications. My arm had slowly started to feel better after being put on an anti-seizure drug, two weeks before my surgery.

If my arm is beginning to feel slightly better and I'm having surgery in four days, maybe I should stop taking ALL the meds now? I wonder what would happen?

I could focus on nothing but getting myself better so I could go back to work. Mamabargains needed its CEO, and it needed her healthy and functional.

Still terrified, but knowing it was the last resort, the night before surgery, I decided that I would still go in, but that I needed to talk to the surgeon before he cut me open.

I had the overwhelming feeling that I was never going to return after surgery. The night before, I wrote heartfelt letters to my kids and Stanford. I felt like I needed to tell them all goodbye.

In Noah's, the most poignant sentence I wrote, *'please be your dad's best friend.'*

Stanford would need a new best friend if I were gone.

With tears in my eyes, I folded my letters nicely and tucked them away in my drawer. Unless someone was intentionally looking, these letters to the future would remain hidden..

That night, kissing my kids goodnight, my gut told me, *this is the last time I'll see them, these boys of ours, and Stanford. What will they do without me? Will they be okay?*

The smile I gave before they closed their eyes would be the final one they'd ever see from me.

I'd run my fingers through their hair, across the bridges of their noses, a nightly ritual I'd done since their births—one last time.

They'll never have more of these moments with me.

I couldn't cry. I didn't want Noah to see my fear, because I knew it would feed his own.

Noah looked into my eyes, unprompted he sleepily uttered these words, *"Don't worry mom, I'll be dad's best friend."*

I shuddered at what I'd just heard.

It wasn't possible he'd found my well-hidden letters. Even if he had, they were written in cursive, illegible to a seven-year-old.

He understood one thing: I was having surgery in the morning. We explained to him what it entailed, and he was visibly shaken—clearly scared for me, long before that night.

In the moment, I had no words for my little Noah, just an embrace before the tears began to flow.

The emotions I'd experienced in his haunting goodnight kept me mostly awake.

God was on my mind, despite my unwavering disbelief in Him. *Is he real?*

That boy read my heart the way no one had ever done so before.

The universe, not God, is intersecting our life, sending glaring warnings my way. Listen, Jessica.

We arrived at the hospital at noon. I decided that even though there were multiple 'signs' telling me to run for the hills, talking to the surgeon would need to be the decision maker for me.

The Mamabargains office staff was on standby, knowing that I'd be offline for twenty four hours, longer than I'd hoped—but this was, after all, major surgery.

Stanford and I sat in the stark white hospital room. I changed into my frumpy, pale blue gown, and then the nurses began pre-op testing. Blood pressure, pee test, then blood work, temperature, etc.

My temperature read 103.1 solid.

"Are you feeling alright? You have a very high fever," asked the nurse.

"I feel absolutely fine."

The nurse looked at me, and, then down at the thermometer. She glanced over at Stanford and back at me again in confusion. Her apparent befuddlement was unnerving, so I asked if everything was all right.

"I'm going to send another nurse in to take your temp with a different thermometer."

A few minutes later, in came a heavy-set nurse with his shiny new thermometer.

Different nurse, different thermometer...Same temperature: solid 103.1.

"I'm going to send your blood work to the lab to determine what type of possible infection you may have," said the new nurse.

Are you fucking kidding me right now? Another sign? Okay universe—I'm listening.

"And I'll page the surgeon to come in and talk with you as well."

Two hours passed.

I sat there in my gown in the cramped pre-operation room while Stanford snored like a freight train in the super uncomfortable looking (but according to the delightful rhythms of his heavy breathing, cozy enough) chair in the corner. My scheduled surgery had long since passed. The waiting was miserable. It only fed my lucid trepidation.

The nurse finally came back in, "Your tests are clean. There's no infection. I have no explanation for your mystery fever." One last check with their thermometer confirmed what we already knew, that this fever of mine was still registering 103.1.

Just then, my spinal surgeon joined us.

After I explained my hesitations and asked about the medications I'd stopped taking, the Doctor said, "Jess, if more people would just listen to their bodies the way you are in this moment, there'd be less regret in life, especially when it comes to surgery. Your body is healing itself. In other words, you *should* run for the hills. I'm proud of you for listening to your body. Do not go through with this. Too many things are telling you not to."

Holy hell!

I ripped that gown off so fast! I smiled as we speed-walked out of the pre-op area.

I felt absolutely alive.

I didn't care that my left arm was literally skin and bones. The damage was finally a physically visible presence. I had little to no muscle mass left in it, but I was alive and well, and I wasn't bringing home a hunk of metal in my neck, either.

I couldn't care less that I'd wake up forever feeling like I'd slept on my neck wrong. And it didn't matter that the range of motion in my neck would be half what it was before the herniation...I felt like I'd cheated death, somehow.

I avoided surgery and learned something that day.

If my arm could heal, and my muscles eventually recover, that certainly it was possible, for Mamabargains to heal too.

Or—it was quite possible that all of those pain drugs had gone to my head and I was just out of my goddamn mind.

We were beyond financial ruin—nothing more to give.

The Singer family was tapped. Health was suffering, marriage and family on the rocks.

We'd lost well into the seven digits in revenue in the year of YUITS. In the end, our family carried more than half a million dollars in business debt. It was especially alarming in consideration of the hours of our lives I'd dedicated to making the business financially successful—how much of my kids' lives.

On average, I worked sixteen-hour days, 365 days a year, for almost six years. I spent more than 35,000 hours dedicated to Mamabargains. That's equivalent, for a regular full-time job, to almost *seventeen years* of work.

I'd done it in just six.

I don't need judgment. I was hard enough on myself. Entrepreneurs *all* work this hard, not just the Singer Family.

Stanford and I reflected on parenthood, on our three boys and the value that their lives gave us versus what we provided for them in return.

We considered what 'Owner' of Mamabargains really meant. Would continuing on take even more from us, from the kids?

We thought about our staff. A big reason we worked so hard.

Tricia, the Warehouse Manager lost her previous job when they suddenly closed. Their employees were met with a sign on the door, no face-to-face notice. I couldn't do that. Tricia was the sole breadwinner for her family. Plus, I was kind of scared of her wife!

Then there was our new tech whiz Ben. I wish we'd found him sooner. He helped us uncover so many of YUITS' dirty deeds. Ben was the sole provider for his young family. Not to mention, he'd just beaten cancer.

Warehouse girl Stephanie had been laid off several months prior. I brought her back when we thought we'd recover. She'd have to go—again. I'd miss the kind smiles she offered, and that pink hair of hers.

Angela was the best Customer Service person we'd ever had. She was a gem, so dedicated. A no-drama single mom who I'd found a kinship with from very early on. We were the same age, and ironically, graduated the same year from high schools across town from one another up in Washington State. Our customers adored her, and so did I.

Bridget was our only Vendor Relations Sales person in the end. A single mom with two daughters that had gone through a nasty divorce the year prior. We celebrated with her when she courageously left the abusive relationship. What a find she was—if only we'd found her sooner.

Gregg hadn't been paid in over a year. He wouldn't bill us. He and I spoke daily for almost six years. He was my work husband, in a way, and I'd miss him dearly. Gregg was a new dad and newlywed. He lost his mom to cancer and his wife was diagnosed with cervical cancer just a few months before we closed. I wasn't certain what we did to deserve his sacrifices, but I was grateful.

There was an outstanding invoice on our books for our PR team. We owed them too. We couldn't pay them.

I was embarrassed by our disintegration.

We even owed the stay-at-home-mom moderators who managed our social media accounts. I wondered if they'd forgive us?

Our business attorney would hate me. I'm so sorry, Margaret. We even owed her.

The vendors. Of nearly a thousand of them, Mamabargains was indebted to just under thirty for previous sales. It killed my soul to know that we'd worked so hard for Mamabargains to be a reputable business, and how quickly it all fell apart.

Finances ebb and flow. They rise and fall. That's a normal part of running a business. We kept hoping against the odds that the dwindling numbers would recover as we battled day in and day out to fix the terrible situation YUITS had left us in. What goes down must come up again at some point, right?

Most importantly, there were the Mamabargains customers. Our lifeblood. Customers whose orders we'd have to cancel if we decided to close, purchased products we wouldn't be able to refund them for. Families living on tight budgets would feel the pinch even more because of us if we opted to shut the doors.

There was no money left with which to refund. Not a dime.

There was no way out of the mess without leaving hurt behind.

We were living in the pinch ourselves. In the small, sweaty, tight space between your ass cheeks—the dark stinky place where shit comes from. We knew the pain.

And ass crack space doesn't give much breathing room. It just stinks.

Agent Lattimer's prognosis had been agonizingly accurate.

We'd been in business three weeks shy of six full years when our minds were made up on that family camping trip to Sand Hollow, Utah.

And as I began the inevitable post mortem soul-search, I at last realized the truth with absolute clarity—I knew in my heart that I couldn't have it all.

I was a business mom with three boys under age eight at home— my real life shit show paled in comparison to the entrepreneurial duties that Mamabargains required of me every day. Could I dig deep, finding more energy to manage both?

Diapers were a part of our daily lives for nine straight years at home.

By my own estimations, I figured at six diaper changes on average per day, until age three for each of our three boys, I'd changed approximately 19,710 diapers in my short and glamorous mom career. Good thing we only had three kid butts to wipe.

How could I possibly have expected to make room for sixteen-hour workdays and diaper changes? Especially when they were most frequently needed on the adult delinquents in diapers themselves, YUITS. Don't they have convalescent homes for that?

To do it all successfully was nearly impossible. I know this with certainty, because I gave it my best for more than 35,000 hours.

The correlation between home and work life, and the crap filled pants that were our daily routine were nothing short of ironic. Not to mention our huge long since passed partnership with Luvs Diapers. Jesus, it was like we'd fallen into a bottomless pit of crap.

Every aspect of our lives brought full force explosive diarrhea our way.

As a mom, no matter the hour of the day or night, wherever you are, be prepared to hear a, 'MOM, COME WIPE MY BUTT!'

And if you don't comply? The punishment and aftermath of your failure to fulfill their request will result in only one thing: feces smeared on every surface of your home.

YUITS and their shit stains were smeared all over our lives.

You don't expect the ass wiping needs to come from your business, but they will. In reality, Mamabargains (YUITS) needed its diapers changed daily. Just like having another baby at home. I wondered, but knew the answer, if Mamabargains would be around to help take care of any feeble fecal needs my elderly years would require.

It was time to pivot.

To clean those up-the-back blowouts caused by business failures and letdowns.

And where would that leave us?

Kids can and will be parasitic little shits, but they'll always love you back. Spousal relationships can be similarly challenging—the best ones will always return your love.

Ask yourself, 'does my business love me back?

Why do owners come back for more when the love is so infrequently returned?

Why had *I* kept coming back?

I had to learn to grow thick, shit-repellent skin. CEO's regularly have people asking for something, needing a piece of them, a slice of their legacy, and a chunk of their time, wanting to be their friend. For a time, I lived for the chaos of it all.

I couldn't give any more of me away. I had to save it for those that mattered the most.

What happens when you no longer have time for the simple pleasures in life?

Like fucking your spouse in peace.

Stanford got fresh with me in our two-year-old's bed once while the kids were all downstairs destroying who knows what.

And I liked it.

We took a detour on the way to our home office, stopping in the first available bed we came across. We snuck down the hall like we were hiding from our own parents. Whisper giggling as we made out, constantly looking up to be sure we didn't hear our three little creepers coming down the hall. Technically it was our room and our furniture, and since the kids live rent free, the least we could do was purify our home with our own, very unique lustration technique—with an emphasis on 'lust'.

Parent-hump. Quick, to the point, rare, enjoyable, and anywhere you can get it.

Even if we only needed eight minutes for a quickie, eight minutes was more than I was able to spare. What mattered more to me? My marriage or my business?

Some fun facts:

Of just twelve years married (144 months), I was pregnant for twenty-seven of those months. And I was sick and puking my guts out for a total of twenty-one months. It took me sixty-two hours of labor to birth my toe-headed small men. And I managed to squeeze in a love affair for seventy-one months with Mamabargains. I didn't even count the time I was on my period and sexy time was off limits. Poor Stanford.

Do the math. What had I left over for my family? My marriage— my kids—that's what really should've meant the most.

I needed to be Jess again, even though sometimes her parenting techniques were as unorthodox as business-Jess's. My always out of the box approach seemed to work for both business *and* personal, though.

One night I pulled out the trailer park Trixie blonde wig from an old white trash Halloween costume, teasing it real nice up top. Damn, I looked good. Pity I didn't have time for sex...or that I was a real blonde. I heard they always have more fun.

It was bedtime for the toddler, and he was having none.of.it.

Skipping Trixie's ice pink lipstick, smeared mascara and neon blue eye shadow, I turned on my phone recorder. Marching down the hall, I cracked our tantrumming toddler's door. Trixie caused just the right level of fear to warrant literal, sudden, and absolute silence from the insane asylum small person flipping me asinine amounts of shit on the other side of the door.

His screaming stopped. Instantly.

Maybe YUITS had just needed Trixie to stop them in their tracks?

I spoke in my best 'blonde wig weirdo mommy' voice, altering it just enough that he was either mesmerized by my sweet, unusual stranger tone, or possibly scared shitless of the blonde bombshell standing in his doorway.

"Fin-leeeeeyyyy, you need to go to sleep, now," I cooed.

"Okay" he said, and did.

That's it? That worked?

I didn't know whether to feel like a clever success or a failure as a parent, but opted to just not give an actual shit because my bed awaited me, and I was happy with any small victory in my sleep-deprived life at that point.

Blonde Wig Mommy visited a few more times, each night successfully coercing our sleep-hating bedtime troll-child to drift off into slumber central.

Parenting is hard fucking work, and you do it however best you know how.

I was doing this whole 'Mamabargains' thing the best way I knew how.

It was time to put big girl pants on, toss out the diapers, and get my real life back.

I wanted more than eight minutes to fuck my husband.

I was going to have to figure out how to deal with this shitty Mamabargains mess one way or another, and I'd need Jessica fully engaged to do so. Daphne couldn't do it, and neither could Mrs. Mamabargains *or* Trailer Park Trixie.

This was different than dealing with a bi-polar dad as a teenager, or the loss of a friend to religion. This wasn't rape or a drug-dealing, cheating boyfriend. This wasn't an ungrateful employee taking advantage, marriage troubles, or problems conceiving.

This was a bomb waiting to explode.

Monday morning, Stanford and I arrived and gathered all the employees.

I felt nausea festering, a pit in my stomach and the urge to pee my pants. The nervous anticipation caused uncontrollable ear ringing. I couldn't hear myself think.

The staff watched us with uncertainty, looking as nervous as I was feeling. We finally had the best staff we could dream of. And it had taken us six years to find them.

We were going to lose them. I wanted to cry-scream. We were family.

"Stanford and I have sadly decided to close Mamabargains. After today, we have nothing left with which to pay any of you. We owe it to each of you to let you know now. The public announcement will come as soon as our attorney tells us we've done everything by the book and can officially, legally close the doors."

With jaws dropped, and a few heartfelt sighs, followed by tears and hugs, it was as if the entire staff enveloped us in one giant embrace. There were no questions. I feared there would be and that I wouldn't have any answers to offer. But they knew we'd done our best, and words weren't necessary.

We thought it could be fixed. In the end, it couldn't.

We gave it our best. It wasn't enough this time.

It was an impossible task, but our personal attorney, Lonnie, tried his hardest to ease the pain. And thank goodness Stanford's insurance at work included legal services, because we'd need a lot of it in the years to come. Thank goodness he'd kept his day job.

"There are always people who are going to be caught in the crossfires. There are no winners when a business closes. Everyone loses— some more than others. You two have lost more than anyone will ever realize," Lonnie said.

Mamabargains had been shit on many times before, by vendors who were paid for product that they never shipped to our customers. I knew what it was like to be taken advantage of. It wasn't our intention for anyone to feel that's what we were doing.

Our objectives were pure, but that didn't stop me from crying myself to sleep nightly for months after closing. I knew we'd failed—we let so many people down.

I'm so sorry we couldn't pay you. We really, truly tried our best.

Through the tears, one thing was clear—I couldn't let my kids down. I had to still be a mom to them, a wife to Stanford. I had to claw my way back and start over again.

My tear soaked pillowcases weren't payment enough for the customers and vendors we left owing—my chest pains, anxiety and body covered in random hives at random times were my problem. I chose to build a business. To grow a business, and to live in the raw sewage it left us drowning in. I needed to accept defeat.

We put a message up on the website and social media pages the day Lonnie said, "You've officially filed the documents required in the State of Utah to legally dissolve the business. All bank accounts and credit cards are closed. The business is no more. Do no more, pay no more, ship no more, cease all business related activities immediately."

But it's never quite that simple.

Until that moment, we had to remain business as usual, liquidating everything we physically had and paying everything we could possibly pay.

You'll never know how difficult it was to keep the business going those few days while we waited for the 'paperwork', the final go-ahead, the 'okay, you can officially announce you are closed.'

We still had two years left on our warehouse lease. That meant we'd owe our landlord, Kim, the remainder on our contract—nearly 100 grand.

Ultimately, Kim let us out of the contract. He'd watched us grow in his warehouse space for years, seeing happy customers as they left our building with smiles on their faces. He hugged me with tears in his eyes when I asked for his forgiveness on the remainder of our lease. I explained our situation, and hoped he'd understand.

"Jessica, it breaks my heart to see you and Stan going through this. I've watched you put everything into Mamabargains. You brought light to the mom industry. I sure hope you write a book about your journey, even the bad parts of it, and when you do, I'd like to read it," Kim said to me, bringing tears to my own eyes as he spoke the words.

"I've been writing throughout my journey for the past six years. I'll be sure to send you a signed copy when it's published," I said, prompting a sincere smile across his face.

There are good-hearted people in this world. Kim is one of them.

My eyes had only been focused on the horrible people, the YUITS of the world. It blinded me to the kind ones just waiting with an outreached hand to help.

There were the shipping and utility companies. We couldn't pay them.

The personal guarantees, like the warehouse lease and the banks were exorbitant.

There was the IRS. We owed them for the last quarter of business taxes. We'd never even paid them late, now we couldn't pay them at all. We owed State taxes as well. How would we come up with more than half a million dollars to pay everyone off?

The business hummed for nearly five years, never in the negative—only positive cash flow until YUITS came along. We tried floating it ourselves that last year—thinking we'd eventually recover.

The final days of a ~~dying~~ dead business are absolute pandemonium.

I wasn't prepared because it was all happening so fast.

The message we posted on the website was met with mixed reviews.

Where to begin...at the beginning—Mamabargains LLC started 6 years go, before any other one deal at a time deal site for mom, kid and baby existed. MB helped to spearhead the deal site revolution. Along the way, we gained so much understanding, support, and many happy years with our loyal fans. The time has come for us to close. Many of you may not know that the company was founded by a stay at home mom, with the savings she and her husband had. There were no investments. There was no capital. There was only them, and over time, many wonderful people who worked for MB and who worked with MB. Throughout the past 6 years, many people have touched their lives, many will remain a part of their lives forever. They have gone through business heartaches, life heartaches, and have sadly come to the devastating decision to close down their baby, Mamabargains LLC. Please be patient with them through this difficult time, and for the 6 years of support, they thank you from the bottom of their hearts.

With Love Always,

The Mamabargains LLC Family

There was disbelief from sad customers 'Mama! Say it isn't so! You're my favorite deal site of them all!' or, 'I've been shopping your site since my children entered the world, you will be greatly missed!' or, 'Best customer service I've ever had—hands down! Thank you for your hard work, you will be missed!'

Inevitably, cynical anger from others, 'Am I going to get the last order I placed? No wonder you went out of business!' or, 'You suck, Mamabargains.'

The angry ones cut deep, but the positive's far outweighed them.

The vendors offered their share of sadness, 'My company would be nowhere near it's size without Mamabargains offering our products to its customers. Thank you from the bottom of our hearts for caring for our brand. You'll be sorely missed.' They also shared their dismay, 'Are we getting paid for our last deal?' or, 'You'll PAY for this.'

Little did they know, we'd already more than paid—tenfold. Just in other ways.

It's impossible to please everyone. In this situation, there was no question my mixed emotion, melting pot brain was in a million different places all at once. Did we make the right decision? How will this impact my family? Our employees?

There was nothing mixed about the last remaining employees, though. They blew us away with one more act of collective kindness and incredible loyalty.

Without pay, each of them stayed through the last week of Mamabargains' life as we liquidated, trying to make sense of what's required when you shutter your business.

There were no support groups for businesses going under. Closing caused more than embarrassment—it was the epitome of devastation for our family. For me.

Like being a first time parent with no rulebook to follow, shutting the doors to business was *far* more stressful than running one. There are loose ends, and no real direction on how to tie them all up. My years of winging it would come in handy as I had to do just that through the entire diabolical process of closing.

My hatred for YUITS became an obsession. They were in large part, if not solely, the cause of the Mamabargains collapse.

And why hadn't I figured that out in time?

What we discovered months after closing would only add to our rage and frustration with YUITS and their lies. I wanted to make those assholes pay. They stole the heart of Mamabargains, along with our good, solid reputation.

On our last day in the building, Stanford and I cleaned. Our oldest and youngest played with a box of their old toys that we'd always kept in the lobby for our customers' children. Our six-year-old monkey sat on the handicapped railing, watching us load boxes of awards into the car. He was in awe of this big building and the cool things that went on inside it, too young to grasp the devastation that was packed inside each of those boxes.

And then our little monkey fell.

Eli was left dangling upside down, with a gnarly leg break right below his kneecap. The only thing keeping him from crashing head first into the concrete below was his mangled left leg, pretzel-wrapped around the railing.

With our child screaming in agony, I smile-cried, running to his rescue. I could finally be the mom that my kids deserved to have—one that would be physically there to untangle them from a railing, pick them up if they fall, tell the it will all be okay. A mom that prioritized her kids above everything else—one that was always *there*.

For all the stressful crap and all the insane moments Mamabargains had brought into our lives, I realized in this very moment that closing was absolutely the right decision.

Thank you universe, for giving me that confirmation. I could finally say goodbye to Mama, to Mrs. Mamabargains, forever. The diapers would need to go.

I no longer questioned whether or not closing was the right decision.

Jessica Singer, mom, wife—was on her way back.

The first stop?

The best litigation attorney zero dollars could buy. I was determined to expose YUITS for what they were—frauds.

Actually, that was second stop. First stop, The Children's Hospital—that broken leg needed serious attention.

As a certain New York bagillionaire has gloated continuously—he's had his businesses file bankruptcy not once, but *four* times. He brags about using the laws of this country for his own personal gain. Because, why not?

Selfish or smart?

He lives high up in a tower he named after himself looking down upon the poor, insignificant people below, mocking them for their inadequacies. He's rich enough to do his own financing, but not rich enough to avoid multiple Chapter Eleven's?

I bet he wants to run our country someday.

If a rich guy like the old, orange faced, toupee haired horn tooter can't avoid four bankruptcies with his various deep pockets, how can the little guys like me, avoid it?

An intelligent man with a full head of wild white hair, a more genuine smile, and a knack for numbers once said, "Try not to become a person of success, but rather try to become a person of value." Albert Einstein wasn't just about relativity.

He was about giving more than he received, and was a role model of mine.

The man in the tower, the one who looked like he just rolled in a bag of cheesy puffs? He just takes.

In 2014 alone, more than half a million businesses closed in the United States. Of those, more than fifty thousand filed for bankruptcy, according to Statistic Brain's New Business Stats for the year.

That means on average, there are about 1,400 businesses that die *each day.*

That rainy April afternoon, Mamabargains' death became a depressing number.

And I hate numbers, by the way.

I'd fallen short—no longer, by definition, a success.

We met with a bankruptcy attorney, asking our book of questions.

It wouldn't take care of the IRS debt, but personal bankruptcy would take care of everything else haunting us.

It was an attractive option and the pros definitely far outweighed the cons.

To Stanford and I, bankruptcy would've been a cop out—the easiest and most unethical option. We just couldn't go through with it.

We were always hard workers—we'll hard work our way out of this, too.

The closing of a business had become my new more than full time trying job.

Be a person of value, Jess. Just like Uncle Albert suggested.

Unfortunately, people of value pay their dues in other ways. The entire Singer family was grieving the loss of the business and its legacy.

My oldest son cried his eyes out, almost daily, and I didn't know how to soothe him. I was crying as well, but bottling it up inside because I needed to be strong. We'd lost Mamabargains and none of us knew how we'd recover. My three boys, who grew up with the business as part of our family were experiencing loss for the first time in their young lives. We'd all have to adjust.

Heart racing for no reason, I felt as if my brain swelled, an explosion imminent.

My suffering psyche trapped me within my own self-doubt.

My oldest wanted to run Mamabargains someday. He'd come into the office and sit in my chair, pretending to be the CEO. He'd go back to the warehouse and help build shipping boxes. He loved sitting and listening to the sales people on the phone with vendors. His ears were always open. I'd inadvertently crushed my son's dreams.

Now he says he wants to be a developer, so someday he can prevent what happened to Mamabargains from happening to another family. Tomorrow, he'll probably want to be something else, because kids are resilient clever—ambitious.

Where was *my* resiliency? *My* ambition?

Scrape to find your self-worth again, Jessica—its there, if you'd just look a little harder.

I wished that closing were as simple as taking a beating from a drug dealing ex, wrapping up a six figure marketing partnership, or cutting it all off and possibly destroying the futures of my children...

But it wasn't.

There were too many decisions that needed to be made, no order to our lives.

I need something to dull the non-stop pounding in my head.

The file folder I kept of the people we owed, and of all the bills piling up eventually surpassed the size of the YUITS folder, glaring at me from the dining room table. It needed resolution.

Beside it, lurked my worry rock. Surrounding me, were sixty-four boxes filled with packing slips, vendor information, employee folders, contracts, and purchase orders.

The burden inside those boxes was heavier than financial stress we were facing.

Where would the money come from?

Mom and Dad, who had none?

Another bank loan?

Just turn the damn phone off. It's never a personal call. It's always a collector, and they're not interested in your excuses.

I couldn't work. Ceasing business operations isn't as final as it sounds, and three kids were a full time job. We couldn't afford daycare.

Maybe I could take Daphne out for a few more spins round the stripper pole?

No. For a start, I'm certain the kids wouldn't gain anything educational from my purple pasties.

And, then, of course, there was me, and the didn't-seem-pressing but should've been issue of my ~~psychological health, OCD, hyper manic~~ mental stability.

Or lack, thereof.

You know, I heard it's *completely* normal for business owners to do an in-depth private investigation prior to hiring consultants. Going into relationships on the premise of distrust, yeah, that's the way to run a company. No sarcasm intended, no, not at all.

I couldn't stop the self-blame pattern. It was my fault for hiring the YUITS sons-of-bitches in the first place. The anger with them fueled my every emotion and action.

The panic attacks and anxiety worsened, leaving no choice but to turn to Zoloft again. I don't think Zoloft is supposed to be used like the latest yo-yo diet craze, right? But I couldn't see, or think straight.

Although we made the ethical decision to close the way we did, that meant we owed six figures in personal debt, and that meant the collection agencies soon came knocking, calling, and harassing us.

Noah came frantically running inside, welling with tears, "Mom, there's a scary guy outside taking pictures of us on the swing."

What?! I looked out the window and there he was, creepy-collector-man taking pictures of our home. What's worse—he'd done it while our *kids* had been playing in *their own* yard.

We hadn't lived beyond our means before the closure. Now? You want my maxed out mortgage with no available equity? We don't own a boat, or a swimming pool, or have some prime parcel of property somewhere near a lake. We have nothing.

No, now we're in over our heads—in the weeds.

And you can't sell my kids, either.

Not today.

I wondered what the neighbors would think of our family.

Who cares what other people think. You worked hard.

The paranoia, a siege mentality set in. I'd call my attorney and he'd send letters. I'd pop more Zoloft and peek out the cracks of the windows waiting for the next collector to approach my door. Our lights were all off— literally and figuratively. We had nothing. You want some plants, some weeds from our yard? That's all we had.

Take the fucking weeds! *Please*!

Should we move? Downsize?

Welcome to our Catch-22.

Good credit is required to qualify for a loan, and ours was shot.

To get a good score you need to have little debt, and ours was astronomical.

We were chained at the base of this looming mountain of debt, an avalanche headed straight for us. Perched on top, was that guy up in his tower, looking down on the little people, like Stanford and I, cackling, making fun of the failures below him.

There's no escape. Help! We can't get out of this—we'll be buried alive!

Yes! Yes, you say. If you've been there, you get it.

Our house was hardly a mansion—we'd taken out the remainder of the equity in order to pay some of the creditors that we had personally guaranteed loans with. If we lost the house, our credit score would be so bad we wouldn't qualify for another.

Dreadful thoughts constantly jostled each other for attention...

We are going to end up homeless.

What if the roof caves in? How would we fix that?

What if the kids need orthodontic work?

During those hopeless days, months, years when the collectors kept coming, I often thought that maybe we'd made the wrong choice in deciding against bankruptcy. Facing up to our debts was ethical, but also exhausting and terrifying.

Goddamn it. Why didn't we just give in and file the Chapter 7?

We had to find cash, and fast.

I'd make trips to kids' consignment shops—offloading some of their old clothes and toys. Even if I just made $13 that would buy us some more potatoes and noodles. I listed everything I could think of on eBay just to pay the power bill. Hawking shoes, jeans, even old bridesmaid dresses that collected dust in the back of my closet. Anything that I could think of to keep the family fed.

I wonder if I could sell my soul on eBay?

Clothes were washed a quarter as frequently. I didn't want expensive water wasted so the toilets were rarely flushed. The Singer family motto was: "If it's yellow, let it mellow, when it's brown, flush it down."

I couldn't justify turning the sprinklers on so our grass and plants outside died. We no longer even had weeds to offer—even they were dead.

Despite our obvious plight, our friends were expecting a comeback. I'd constantly be asked, "What's next for you, Jess?"

"I'm really into non-profit work, now," I'd say.

They probably didn't grasp the dark humor in my double-entendre. It became an inside joke I only shared with myself.

At one point, my parents gave us a cash card so we could pay for a hotel—a getaway for the weekend for a family that couldn't afford to pay for their own *anything*. It was such a generous gift from a couple that sacrificed so that we could have a break from the tedium of debt.

Thanks mom and dad, but I'm sorry to tell you we didn't go away that weekend like you hoped.

We bought groceries instead with the cash card. We'd been out of milk for weeks. The car needed gas. My trips to those consignment shops added up in burnt fuel. I spent $24 in gas to make $19.

We owed so much to other people, but had to keep our life afloat. We didn't want the kids to see our financial struggles. But they knew.

While we grew fundamentally poorer post-close, the kids grew abundantly richer.

We wanted consistency for them. And they had it (us)—we just hadn't realized it was Stanford and I being more present all along.

The letters continued to come, the emails, and the messages on Facebook, LinkedIn, and on Twitter. Everywhere I could be found online, the angry vendors and customers made their voices heard. They didn't realize that they were already weighing heavily on my mind. They didn't need to send me angry words for that to happen.

I fed myself angry words every day.

A knock on the door only two months after we closed and there stood a uniformed Constable armed with an envelope. I'd let my guard down and was expecting a friend that afternoon. Instead, I received an aggressive, "You've been served!"

Why does he look disgusted with me?

He doesn't know us, he has no idea.

The letter contained a lawsuit that a vendor was filing against us for the very last deal we'd run with them. We knew it was going to come. And they clearly didn't know we didn't have the roughly $3,000 that was owed.

Three grand? We didn't have three bucks. We'd worked with this vendor for six years, and now the strong relationship that we built with them ended in flames.

A few weeks later, there we were in the Sandy City, Utah Courthouse, seated directly across from the suing vendor. I looked at the plaintiff intently, willing the universe to turn her head my direction. If only she could lend me a moment of contact with her eyes, she'd see the hurt and apology in mine.

The law sided with us, with Mamabargains LLC, because we had nothing to give. Our priority debts were with the IRS, and with the personal guarantees. Though the vendor hadn't seen my emotion-filled eyes, the judge must've taken note.

We didn't personally guarantee the amount owed to the customers and vendors, so they'd all have to take it as a loss on their books.

"You're attempting to sue a company, Mamabargains LLC, that has been legally dissolved in the State of Utah. That's like trying to sue a dead person buried in the ground," said the judge. "Furthermore, there was no contract they signed with you personally guaranteeing this debt. The debt is with Mamabargains LLC, and that company is no more."

I was a hypocrite—using the laws of this country to our benefit, just like the orange-faced-troll in the tower had. Only, I wasn't proud of it, like he was. I was protecting my family, not my business.

Forming an LLC when we started Mamabargains in 2008 was smart. It gave us personal protection in the event the business closed. It was the only silver lining on the pitch-black cloud I could find, but it wasn't much of one at that.

After the judge made his bittersweet ruling, the vendor approached Stanford and I.

Even though we'd won, I felt terrible for her, embarrassed by the situation itself.

"I'm so sorry. Closing was never our intention. I hope you can see that. My family lost more than just our business when we closed. I feel awful you were caught in the middle."

Her response?

She hugged me.

Standing back, one hand on each of my shoulders, she breathed in our devastation. She held my eyes, weak to the core, tightly within her own.

The time in the courtroom brought up all of the reasons for our closure. The judge saw my file on YUITS along with our personal financial records. It was clear to him, and now to everyone else that the situation had taken more from us than we were able to give.

I wonder how long before the bank forecloses our house? It's already months late. Business credit card payments are due. The kids' reading glasses will have to wait.

"Jessica. I'm sorry it came to this—the lawsuit. It was just business. I had no idea the depth of what was happening, or the circumstances of why you closed. I just didn't know, and I'm very sorry for your loss. You're forgiven. I wish you and your family the absolute best— you have a long road ahead of you," said the vendor, reminding me one more time that there are good people in this world.

She was right. This *was* going to be a long road, and we weren't prepared.

I received more than twenty phone calls a day from collectors, and I spoke to each of them, explaining what happened and why we couldn't pay. Some took our explanation and never called again, and some persisted and kept harassing us multiple times a day.

The collection calls and letters only increased in frequency, and I had no idea what I was in for emotionally.

Tenacious Jess was losing steam.

The banks were the most aggressive.

When times were great at Mamabargains, we'd funded much of our marketing efforts by taking on personally guaranteed bank loans, leaving the liquid cash flow for reinvestment into new products, payroll and website development.

We learned a lesson there: Never personally guarantee *anything* in business. Ever.

Long after our close, we were paying for the marketing efforts of a company that was no more, out of our empty pockets.

It was summer, and I had one kid home with a broken leg and no idea how we'd pay the associated medical bills that would inevitably follow. Eli was casted for eight weeks, and couldn't even get himself up the stairs on his crutches.

So I carried him.

I carried him when he had to pee or poop or eat. When he wanted to play with his toys upstairs. When he needed to go to bed at night and when he woke up in the morning.

That's what parents do, and that's what CEO's do. They carry it.

I was carrying him physically. Simultaneously, I allowed the weight of the business closure dealings to rest on my shoulders while Stanford worked ten-hour days. He did his best to clock out of the mess, working hard to try to pay back our debts. And when he got home, he was exhausted. Ready to recharge, to go to sleep and then do it all over again the next day. And the next...

I wondered, who'd be there to carry *me*?

I'd listen to him peacefully sleep-snoring next to me, disconnecting it—me, us.

I need to talk about all of this! How can you sleep right now?

I resented his emotional on-off switch.

If he could shut off, maybe I should too...

Permanently.

Three weeks after Mamabargains collapsed, so did I.

Adjusting to life after its death was killing me.

It all came crashing down in mid May 2014.

It kicked off with an absolute, fucking lunatic-laced mental-breakdown screaming-match with my only confidant Stanford—while our children slept down the hall. At least I hope they were sleeping and didn't hear what their crazed Mom was spewing at their patient Dad.

I don't remember how it began, or why.

I do know that I didn't have one single reason to explode with anger and agony—I had a million.

I spent so much of my life taking care of everyone around me that I'd somehow forgotten how to take care of me. I'd neglected my mental and physical health, for too long.

And historically, when I had no one to take care of?

I'd find someone—something—I'd find a 'project'.

I found Jake. He needed someone to take care of him, the drug addict he was.

There was Marie—the innocent, God-obsessed once upon a time best friend of mine. She'd needed me because her parents suffocated her with their rules...and then she gave in to their claustrophobic helicopter parenting and dumped me in the process.

I can't forget Kevin, the rapist. I adequately cared for his repulsive needs—unwillingly so, and then kept my mouth shut, his shameful crime forever a secret for me to bear.

There was my family—my brothers, my mom and dad. I did my best as the oldest kid in the family to nurture my little brothers. I tried to shelter them, even though no one expected me to, so Mom could work overtime, and Dad could have his connection with Jesus.

Then there were those like Becca, Jane, Hailey and others I've encountered in their wake. I let them walk all over me—because I *needed* to be needed.

Now?

Now I was the loser. I was taking care of my kids the best I could, but it felt I was shouldering the burden like a solo parent would.

The trouble was, Stanford was damaged, too. Suffering beneath his stoicism, he put on a good demonstration of strength, never letting on to weaknesses I knew he had, but refused to show.

He monetarily carried the burden alone, balancing the monkey on his back weight of our family's livelihood. Financial freedom had always been a life goal of ours. After the close, it seemed out of reach with the catastrophic money mess that Mamabargains left us with.

Perhaps the vacant look Stanford always had was his real stress coping mechanism. Either way, he was pushing me away. My family, my kids and marriage were all I had left. These were the things that I hoped would carry me when I needed it most, what gave our life value and meaning—the real things that made us rich.

I gave as much as I could. If you asked Stanford, he'd tell you that I'm not a selfish person. He'd say that I *should* be more selfish, that I should take more time for *me*, do more things for *me*.

I didn't know how. To take care of myself, that is.

I was constantly harassed by the feelings of isolation and loss—hunted by debt collectors.

Stanford and I went at it. It was the worst fight we'd ever had in our ten years of marriage.

I'd make 'hitting rock bottom' more than just a metaphor.

I felt a visceral urge to pull a Thelma & Louise in that moment, except I didn't exactly have a Louise to accompany me over a cliff—and the car was fresh out of gas. Again.

Pathetic. I can't even afford the gas the car needs to drive off the mountain's edge.

"I can't do this *alone*, Stanford! We're falling apart and where are you? You haven't looked at me in weeks. You get up and go to work, clocking out of your family and out of this mess, leaving me to pick up the pieces here at home by myself," I said, heart pounding so loud, blood boiling hot, I was flush with scarlet-mad, burning cheeks.

"You go to bed at night, closing your eyes like this problem isn't staring at *both* of us!"

In another first and worst for our marriage, my words made the usual calm Stanford angry.

"Do you want to *trade*, then? Why don't I stay home with the kids and you can go get a job that will pay for all the bills *and* for the Mamabargains debt that's now hanging over our heads!" Stanford picked up a pillow and flung it at the wall.

Thankful that it wasn't something heavier or more damaging he'd decided to heave across the room, I was beginning to see the pain he was also in.

Show that pillow who's boss, Stan—*own* that pillow, you big softie, tough-guy wannabe.

Stanford, my sweet man of a husband wouldn't hurt a fly. He's not the guy you want backing you up in a bar. He hates conflict and shies away from it. Yes, now he was having a verbal argument with me, and a physical fistfight with a pillow.

And he was winning.

"That's not practical, Stanford! You know when I was working grueling sixteen-hour days at Mamabargains, and you were working part time at your engineering job, free to mountain bike or snowboard or golf at your leisure? You *had* time to yourself—you had *freedom*. I had *none*. I buried myself in work so that *you* could work *less* and play *more*. It was all hunky-dory when the money was coming in, but *now*, now that *I'm* not bringing in that dough, now it's all on *me?"*

It was at this point that I noticed the high-pitched, shrill screaming coming from my mouth.

"No, I mean...I know that you worked hard, but..."

"But? But this is something we are supposed to be going through *together*, working through—*together.* But you aren't *here*, and I don't mean physically, I mean *emotionally*! I'm about ready to lose it. I'm losing myself here, Stanford. IT'S NOT GOING TO BE PRETTY!"

"Our only choice is for me to deploy," Stanford said, point blank.

"Excuse me?" I said, confused. We'd discussed it before, but decided against it.

The Middle East job was a once in a lifetime opportunity to help ease the burden on at least half of the total debt to just the banks—the personal guarantees.

But there was one major issue with the engineering gig in the desert.

It was in fucking war-torn *Afghanistan*.

We'd talked about it before this night, before this blow up fight of ours, and I thought it was settled. Stanford's life was worth more than the debt of Mamabargains. I'd never forgive myself if anything happened to him there on account of business debt here.

His family would never forgive me, either. They always found a way to blame me.

"So that's it. You're not just going to clock out for the day, you're going to clock out for *four* months? And you're going to go live in fucking *hell* while your family hopes they get to see you safe and sound on US soil again?"

But, he was right. It was either the war zone, or bankruptcy. Even with this dangerous option, we wouldn't be able to pay it all off. This man, this husband of mine was going to risk his life for what? Stanford made this decision for his family, to help save us from bankruptcy—and to save us from each other. He didn't want to take the cowardly way out. A bankruptcy would've wiped the slate clean, but was the least morally sound way out.

I was enraged that he was right, scraping for any excuse for him to stay, but I knew that it was the best thing for our family, and that's what parents do. That's what CEO's do. They make sacrifices. They carry it.

Stanford decided to make this sacrifice and needed support I wasn't sure I could offer.

It was below forty degrees outside, uncharacteristically cold for a May in Utah, and I only had on a long sleeve shirt and jeans.

Without a word, or a second thought, I slipped my flip-flops on, leaving Stanford standing at the bottom of the stairs. I didn't turn to look at him, only offering my backside as I walked straight out the front door, abandoning my life and everything in it.

I didn't turn because I didn't want to see his disappointment.

I clocked out, because if he could, than so would I.

I needed a life escape.

I had no idea where I was going to go—we had no family in Utah, and I wasn't going to involve any of our friends in this meltdown of ours... This meltdown of *mine*.

Alone with just my own thoughts, I walked hard and fast, no real destination in mind.

Don't let this take you, Jess. Be stronger than this shit. Walk it off.

I was freezing, and all I had with me was my phone, and it was almost dead.

I was hysterically crying, and my thoughts were so scattered, because I hadn't realized it before, but this was the night that I *did* hit rock bottom. I was so empty inside, so alone, so scared. Just absolutely terrified of the too many 'what-if's' that faced our family.

I didn't need any fucking help—and even if I *did*, I'd never have asked for it. That wasn't my style. It never has been and never will be. I'd find my way home by myself, when I was damn ready. I had to climb out of this depression alone.

A few years prior, a local restaurant business near our house had gone through a tumultuous lawsuit. Something about an old business partner suing the owners for millions. The old business partner won the contract dispute, and only weeks after the ruling, the owners, a 56-year-old husband and his 57-year-old wife, took their own lives on Christmas Day 2010. The news called their deaths a murder- suicide.

I call it a tragedy.

When the tragedy happened, Mamabargains was rocking. Everything was rainbows and unicorns for us at the time. I couldn't understand how any sort of business issue could push a human to such extremes. They had a family—kids, *grand*kids. They had each other.

Now, though, all alone on this chilly night, it wasn't hard to fathom why they did it. There was devastation all around them. The embarrassment and overwhelming feelings of failure vanquished them, and I acknowledged their loss quietly. Unlike when the tragedy occurred, living in this moment of agony I deeply understood what they'd gone through.

I wanted to scream at the top of my lungs, but I had no voice. So my brain wailed inside my pounding head instead.

I abused myself with words I'd never speak aloud to anyone.

You horrible person. You failure. You idiot. Just do it. Take yourself from this Earth. No one wants you. No one really needs you. The world will be a better place without you.

I found myself sitting on a rock at the dead couple's restaurant property, at nearly 2am, gazing out at the beautiful grounds, the pond, the chateau. I was looking across at the amazing accomplishment they'd built with their hands and had grown into one of the most successful restaurants in Salt Lake City. It slipped away from them, and *they* slipped from their family.

I entered a kind of darkness, a bottomless pit I'd never entered before. It was the deepest crevice of my own mind. And I didn't have an escape plan. Maybe I'd stay here in this still moment on this slab of rock forever.

Maybe I'd need something stronger than Zoloft.

I'd definitely need a therapist.

Either way, I had three kids at home and a husband who maybe wasn't as worried about me as I hoped he would've been. I'd been gone nearly two hours and didn't take my car or even my wallet. He knew I needed space, but why hadn't he stopped me from leaving? Why hadn't he called me yet? This wasn't like me, to disappear like this. Who was going to make me their project? Where was *my* Jess?

Wait. I was right. This *wasn't* me. It wasn't me at all. I was intelligent, loving, kind, unselfish. What the fuck am I doing, wandering the night like some crazed maniac?

Get a fucking grip, Jessica. Get it together. You're losing it. Don't let this destroy you. You love your husband, and you adore your kids, don't leave things like this. Don't leave them.

And then it hit me...

Jess? You gotta save yourself!

I looked down at my phone with its remaining 2% battery. The precise moment my eyes made contact with the screen, a message came through:

"Please come home. I'm worried about you. I love you."

And like the snap of a finger, reality reappeared in front of me. This night, this breakdown, and devastation—I knew it would pass. Stanford and I were good at being on the same page, we'd somehow thought about each other at exactly the same time. I used that moment of digital synchronicity to climb out of the hole.

Thanks for throwing me that rope, Stanford. Your message saved me—again.

Breathe, Jessica. Just breathe.

The walk home didn't seem as long. I'd put distance between the ones that saw me for all of my frailty, and loved me not in spite of it, but *because* of it.

I began to run. Not just because my fingers were turning a new shade of purple from the cold night, but also because I needed to see Stanford, to embrace him and thank him for all he'd done for our family over the years. I wanted to be there to kiss my kids that night and every night after.

And in the morning?

I hoped a therapist was available...

I had nearly thirty years worth of shit to talk about.

I didn't care if he snored while he slept, at least he was there, *next to me.*

It was a done deal. No turning back.

The decision was made and the money he'd earn was already spent Stanford would be leaving for his position in the desert of hell.

Wells Fargo, Bank of America, Capital One, the IRS, the State of Utah, they'd each get their share of my husband's life-risking income.

Our family? We'd have little left over to live on.

Stay at home momming became my every day energy sucker. I'd done it when Noah was a baby, never thinking I'd revisit it again. But there I was, neck deep in ABC's, hide and seek, building forts and riding bikes. I wanted to enjoy the time with our boys, I really did, but I spread myself too thin. I was still tying up loose ends of the business, constantly fielding the demands for the money we didn't have with the demands of my three half-pint bosses asking for another PB&J.

Who dug up our money tree? And who drew on the wall again?

Where is this magic money the banks think we have? Please show me!

I should've been surprised when fate dumped on us yet again. But I wasn't.

And there are tougher things in life. I learned that in the months after our closing. Things could always be worse—get worse.

Only weeks before Stanford left for the desert, I started my period—again. I was accustomed to the irregular visits from Aunt Flo. The difference this time is that it didn't *stop*. Flo stuck around, wearing out her welcome. She lasted three months before I decided something needed to be done.

It was at the same time that we said farewell to Stanford. The goodbye at the airport was more painful than I could've ever imagined. Watching my two oldest boys be destroyed by their own flowing tears, brought up a raw emotional calamity within myself. There was no way of hiding it and we all understood one thing clearly—this could be the last time we ever laid eyes on Stanford. He could walk away and Afghanistan could take him from us, forever.

We watched him walk towards the terminal, and with one last turn, he waved our direction. I was reminded of the meltdown night I left him only weeks before and wondered if his heart sunk that night the same way mine was in that moment at the Salt Lake City airport.

The reality of his farewell made the thirty-minute silent drive home with my kids positively raw. The three-year-old offered sound advice to his bawling family members, "Guys, dad's just going on vacation! Don't cry!" and "Stop crying. It's annoying." I could do nothing but smile in that moment, he was so young—so naïve.

Don't let your mind go there. There's no room in your lives for this darkness.

I hoped there wouldn't be a time that I'd have to explain to the boys why dad left and why he was taken from us too young. My heart hoped that this airport goodbye wasn't the last memory they'd have of their dad—or me of my husband. I had to carry my kids through this and know that there was no one left in Utah to carry me. I'd be going it all alone, now. I needed strength, especially with the emergence of my latest health issue.

I said a universal prayer, to no one in particular, because I believe you receive what you give, what you 'put out' there, and that God fellow didn't seem to like me much.

Persistence and patience—he'll be okay, he'll make it back to you and the boys.

Hello, again, old friend Zoloft. It's me, Jessica. Long time no see!

My on again off again courtship with the anxiety medication had become a crutch for me. Rescuing me when I was at my frazzled wits end, but Zoloft also had its down side. Because it changed me so drastically, the moment I would feel humdrum Jessica visiting, I'd immediately stop taking it. I hadn't taken it in the first few months after we'd closed because I needed command of my fiery edge. Now, I just needed to *be*. I needed to get through these months calmly, and I hoped Zoloft was the answer.

The Zoloft zombie, Jessica, was coming back for a visit.

Every paycheck that came our way, we had another bank payment to make. We couldn't begin the process of settling with them until Stanford was back in the States, so we'd have to keep all of the accounts current on their payments. It took a lot of nickel and diming to get it right—to be sure that each payment was made by the due date to avoid being sent to collections. I had to manage business and personal finances, making sure that the business was current, falling behind on personal bills as a result. Normally, this would be an easy feat, but for a business the size of Mamabargains, combined with the fact that I was now a single mom, I was quickly failing. My brain turning into a rubber-banded ball of madness was the logical next occurrence.

The bleeding persisted.

Just ignore it. It's got to eventually stop, right?

The calls and meetings with our attorney increased in frequency.

Lonnie (our jolly attorney) is probably so sick of me by now.

The collection agency calls grew more frequent, more vicious.

Please stop calling me. Unless you've got a million bucks (or cake, I do like cake), don't stop by either. No one is home. That's not me shhhshing the kids, that's just your imagination.

Stanford's dad came once a month for a weekend and for that, I'll always be grateful. His visit gave the boys something to look forward to each month and me a chance to breathe for a couple of days. He was great with the kids—just what they needed with their dad 7,271 miles away. But who's counting?

My dad also came out for two weeks to help me with house tasks that Stan usually took care of. It gave us a chance to reconnect the father daughter bond that went MIA during the years of his illness. Even in the years following his diagnosis and after the doctors found the right balance of medication for him, we'd lost our closeness. I'd forgotten how much I needed to be daddy's little girl. His composed patience with my three rowdy boys and my teary breakdowns were enough to remind me that my dad still is the most kind, non-judgmental, generous man I've ever known. His humble attentiveness to the human spirit is something I wished would rub off on me more.

When I dropped Dad at the airport, he said, "Love ya, Squirt," the greatest words he could've used to mark the momentous occasion. The biblical Jess-i-ca of yesteryear was gone, for good.

Halfway through Stan's deployment, I decided that the multi-month flow below wasn't normal. I was sick of exhausting half my life in the feminine hygiene aisle at the supermarket. Do you know what its like to consider stealing a box of tampons because you have no money to buy more? Someone really should invent period underwear. Me, *I* should invent period underwear.

My doctors always knew me by name (not proud of that fact). This clearly wasn't my first health crisis rodeo and I knew it wouldn't be my last. I was nervous as hell and really wished Stanford could be there with me physically. At least the appointment fell during a time that Stanford could be with me on Facetime. A virtual date with the doc would have to do. Quite a way to wine and dine your spouse from halfway around the world—with my legs in stirrups, for reasons other than the dirty ones coming to mind.

It didn't take long for the doctor to find some sort of a fibrous looking mass on my left ovary again (I'd had a harmless mass removed several years prior). Even though it appeared benign, combined with the excessive, non-stop bleeding—it needed a resolve.

"Are you two done having kids?" Dr. Watts asked.

"Yes, we were done at two!" I joked, my knee-jerk response to stressful situations. Probably not the right time to crack a funny, but it did enlist a smile from both the doctor and Stanford, so #jessicawin.

"You have two options. We can do an endometrial ablation, in which the lining of your uterus will be destroyed, thus taking care of the bleeding. But, there's still the endometriosis. You won't have a period anymore, but you'll still have the disease, which could be, and is likely the cause of the incessant bleeding. The ablation itself will be just a bandage on the larger issue here, which always comes down to your disease. If you're done having kids, you may want to consider a hysterectomy so the bleeding stops *permanently*, and so we can remediate the endometriosis again."

"So, will I end up in menopause?" I asked.

"We'll remove only what we need to. I hope to leave one ovary so you don't begin menopause at this young age, but we can't make any promises until we get inside and can determine how bad the disease has gotten again. I'll just need your permission to remove everything if we need to."

Ultimately, the choice was made for me ten years before, in December 2004, when I was first diagnosed with endometriosis. After that first surgery so long ago, the surgeon had explained to Stanford and I that I'd be a thirty-year-old hysterectomy candidate. I'd outpaced age thirty by six years, so the uterus removal was long overdue.

Hysterectomy was the only choice.

Add another thing to my growing shit-list.

The surgery couldn't wait. I was miserable. The debilitating, fetal position cramps and the bleeding...the disease was spreading and I didn't need that damn uterus anyway. My three boys needed their mom focused on them, and healthy.

Surgery was scheduled for two weeks later.

Asking for help was never my forte, but I had to put my ego and pride aside.

I called on the two people in Washington I knew would be here for me, no matter what—my mom and my best friend, Elizabeth. Along with the help of my best local friends here, the kids would be taken care of during and after. *We'd all* be taken care of.

I didn't know until I came out of anesthesia that day, November 17th, 2014, that Dr. Watts removed all but the left ovary. It was a bit damaged, but still functional.

Uterusless in Utah.

What am I now? An 'it'? I don't have a fucking uterus.

What did I do?

What is sex going to be like? Humping a sock?

My pretty little reminiscent-of-a-ram looking lady part was deduced to one gonad like ball, commonly referred to as an ovary, and a pouch—*an upside down pouch, you guys.*

A sealed off space that used to make up my entire womanhood is only big enough now for some spare change—if I had any to begin with.

The term 'gutless' carried a whole new meaning to me.

Surgery went well, and I was sent home a day later, in awful pain, feeling like I'd just birthed a reproductive organ.

It was evening but felt like morning. I slept more and probably better than I'd ever slept in my life. I had foggy moments of consciousness and an overall sense of euphoric relief. This was the stuff that makes pill-popping addicts an actual thing.

It was during one moment in particular, I felt overly confident in answering the phone when it rang.

It was my dumb ass moment.

"Hello, this is Jessica," I slurred.

"Hi there. This is your local IRS office. We're calling to let you know we have a revenue officer en route. They'll be at your residence within twenty minutes. They'd like to discuss the debt that Mamabargains owes for one quarter and two weeks worth of back payroll taxes."

Why the *fuck* had I answered that phone?

What was I going to do?

How was I going to prepare for a meeting with the IRS without Stanford there—wait—I'd just returned that same day from *surgery!* Never mind Stanford being gone, I was hopped up on pain meds.

Probably my only coherent thought through the drug induced haze was panic: *this is not going to go well—at all.*

Mom jumped into action, I grabbed my worry rock and got as comfortable as I could on the couch. We begged my three rowdy boys to behave.

The house was chaos in those moments before the IRS guy was slated to arrive. High five to mom for running the gamut on preparations, because I could barely move. Movie and pep talk for the boys—check. A tube of processed crappy cookie dough to woo the IRS man with—check. Thanks, Mom.

Nothing says, *'I'm sorry, please don't sue me or take me to jail'* better than the smell and taste of fresh baked chocolate chip cookies being offered in exchange for my freedom, right? Maybe he'd need a sandwich. *Probably the best way to an IRS enforcer's heart is through his stomach.* Jesus. I had no idea what to do. Mom didn't either, but thankfully she figured it out, because the knock on the door came before we were ready.

My holy-legged, dirty pajamas, hiding my drug-ridden jiggly legs staggered to the front door. My ass of a dog barking behind me couldn't have made the situation worse.

And then I opened the door and there they were.

He was a *she.*

And then the folder of papers flew.

The dog leaped.

The toddler flipped.

My cookie-baking mom supported me from the corner.

The drugs. Dammmmn...the drugs. The drugs were *good.*

The laser-eyed stare of death from the greasy-haired, unkempt *woman enforcer...*

It was all just a precursor to what was to come, to what our resolve would be. The IRS decision that would impact our future all rode on this conversation. I hoped the chaos that she experienced in our living room that day wasn't going to sway her ultimate decision. Or—maybe it should.

A day in the life of the Singers, that's what that day was.

"...I'll take the unabridged version. And by the way, my name is Nancy James."

Thankful to be on a first name basis with her now, I was okay with her turning down the cookies, and the sandwich—even the water. Must be something in their job description about refusing gifts and sustenance.

So I explained. I told her everything, just like I have with you. She asked questions—intrigued. She asked about how the business started, how we marketed it. She asked about our employees and about the first person we fired. She was truly interested in what caused Mamabargains to have its ass handed to it on a silver platter.

She had me log into our online bank accounts—all of them. I showed her our embarrassing balances, nearly negative in our checking, zero in savings, and maxed out credit on the credit cards. I showed her my meticulously tracked spending spreadsheet. Our income was more than ten grand short of the payments we made each month.

And, just like with you, I shared it all. The good, the bad. The successes, the failures. Nancy listened. She didn't treat me the way the banks had. She listened, and she softened.

But we still owed the IRS money, that part, I couldn't explain away.

In the end, Nancy shook my hand, and through my drug induced state, I remember her thanking my mom for being there for me after surgery.

With that, she walked out the front door, leaving us to stew on her last sentence.

"I'll take this information to my superiors tomorrow and will call you soon with the decision the IRS makes on how to best pursue the remainder of the debt that Mamabargains LLC owes it."

By then, we'd paid a quarter of what we owed the IRS, with tens of thousands to go.

And with our necks on the line, as I recovered from the surgery, I obsessed more and more about who'd caused all this shit in the first place. I spoke with several litigation attorneys that all agreed we had a slam-dunk case against YUITS. The lawyers all said they could win the case in their sleep. YUITS' wrongdoing was black and white.

Only—there was a clincher: We'd have to prove that they had *money* to go after.

One of the attorneys offered to hire a private investigator on our behalf to have YUITS investigated, and I agreed, thankful for the olive branch being handed to me.

What they discovered fueled a level of rage I'd never felt before.

As it turned out, YUITS, on paper, had *nothing*.

They'd told us they had four offices around the world—in Seattle, Houston, Salt Lake and one in London.

In reality, we discovered only *one* office.

Their basement office out of their home in Seattle served as their *'headquarters'*. It wasn't even *their* home—it was a house they were *renting*. These guys had bold-faced lied to us, fraudulently representing themselves as much larger than they ever were, and we'd *believed* them. I'd believed them. We discovered they didn't have a business insurance policy, either— but even that is still up for deeper investigation.

Ultimately, these guys were responsible for Mamabargains losing more than two million in revenue, and we'd see a big fat *zero* if we sued them.

I asked the litigation attorney, "But can't we still sue them anyway? You said you could win this lawsuit in your sleep, right?"

"Theoretically, we can go after them, sue them, *and win. But,* then you'd have a judgment in your favor—one that you can't even *collect* upon. You'd pay me my attorney fees since I wouldn't be able to collect from winning the suit either. At the end of the day—this win would look like an asset to you and Stanford, one you wouldn't be able to collect on. You'd have all sorts of people coming out of the woodwork to collect what Mamabargains owed them, simply because it would *look* like you had an asset in the judgment that we'd get in your favor."

"Essentially, winning this lawsuit would only impact you negatively since you'll never see a dime of it."

I shook with impotent rage in his office. I remembered all those other times YUITS had fucked us over and I couldn't contain myself. I wanted to throw that folder filled with YUITS' dirty deeds across the room. I pictured its contents—hundreds of pages representing the million pieces of me that were now scattered and crushed—flying everywhere.

"I'm so sorry, Jess. I know I could win, but it would mean greater loss to you. We could do a more thorough investigation, maybe they're hiding money somewhere. But the reality is that you'll spend money you don't even have and you've already been bled dry from these guys, don't let them take any more from *your family."*

I'm depleted—a dead battery.

"So, what's next for you, Jessica?" he asked, clearly seeing a change of topic was called for.

"Next? I can't see that far ahead. I can't imagine life without Mamabargains, even though I've been living it for a few months now. I'm overqualified for many jobs, and who wants to hire an ex-CEO loser like me, anyway?" I responded, laughing it off like I was making a joke, but fully taking it seriously—*believing* my own words.

That's what I was now—an ex-CEO who let her business fail. I couldn't even succeed at holding responsible the people that took it all away from us.

I hate that question. What's next? Like I'm thinking that far ahead. Or, was I?

And that was it. We'd hoped against all odds that they'd pay for what they did to us. We wanted to prevent them from doing this to another company ever again. Even now, I wish I could just shout from the mountaintops what their real company name is. I don't want to see a company fail, but theirs—theirs deserves failure.

I hate that I feel that way.

We'd been had.

But it was time to move on. Case closed, before it even opened.

When Nancy, the IRS lady called that afternoon, I didn't know whether to pick the phone up or just let it go straight to voicemail. I couldn't handle another let down of epic proportions. I'd already been dealt one huge blow that week, why not go for a record and make it two? She was probably calling to tell me they'd decided to arrest me for non-payment, hat the penalties for non-payment in full would now surpass the total we owed to begin with. The government likes to tax the little guy, don't they?

Because I'm a glutton for punishment, I answered.

"Jessica, hi, it's Nancy. Do you have a few minutes?"

Uh, yeah, let me just put aside my business owner and single mom recovering from surgery duties for a few moments...oh wait, that's right. I don't have a business anymore. I was grateful that for once my filter was working and I didn't say it aloud.

"Sure, Nancy, what's the verdict?"

"On behalf of the IRS, I'd like to tell you that we've decided to *write off* the remaining balance that Mamabargains LLC owes the IRS. You've shown good faith in making payments long after your business closed, and your bank accounts demonstrate clear financial hardship. You've been through enough. We won't add to it. Thank you for always making payments on time, for contributing to our local economic growth through the great 2008 recession. You started your business where many others were closing, and you *thrived*. It was the *right* business at the *right* time, and many others have followed in your footsteps. I sure hope this eases your burden, even if just slightly. And I hope Stanford comes back safe and sound to your family so you can all move forward as one unit, putting Mamabargains behind you."

Nancy was clearly excited to share the wonderful news with me. And wonderful news it was...

I was all alone that afternoon—no one around to share the verdict with. The kids were in school—the preschooler napping. I looked around as I breathed in the impact of the IRS news.

Have I mentioned that there are good people in this world?

Nancy had finished the call with a now familiar, "So, what's next for you, Jessica?"

I'd hated that question before—because I didn't know the answer and felt like I had to have one prepared. It had become the number one query from everyone in the days, weeks and months following the collapse of Mamabargains.

I hated that I had no answer.

"I don't know. I'll let you know when I figure it out," I said with a chuckle.

A few weeks later, on December 31st, 2014, Stanford would be home and we'd celebrate his homecoming with our closest friends in Utah. He'd meet new friends that rallied support for me in his absence—the kids' teachers, parents of their friends. They all knew Stanford was gone, some knew why, others wondered, but didn't ask.

I learned to ask for help when I needed it.

We'd celebrate the end of 2014 and the beginning of a new year—a year that would present it's own challenges for our marriage, our family, and our future. But at least those challenges wouldn't be all about Mamabargains anymore. We still had a long road ahead of us to truly put it all behind us, but at least we could focus on family.

We could be priority to each other again.

Noah, Eli and Finley had their mom and dad back—this time, forever.

We realized through our journey, that it didn't matter what we'd been through, as long as we endured the triumphs, the losses together.

And in the end, I'd hear that infamous question, 'So what's next for you, Jessica?' more than a handful of times over and over again.

And I finally had the answer:

You're holding it.

A Satirical Look At Where They Are Now

Don't let the shit times define you.

In a shocking twist of fate, Jake was shot by his outlaw, gun-toting grandma. She'd done it with the very gun the idiot had stolen years earlier from his grandpa.

Before his death, I heard reports from family and friends back home. Jake, considered 'legally insane', was on permanent disability. The former poet turned drug-dealer apparently believed he was Jesus Christ. I sure am glad he found the Lord before he croaked.

His body is on permanent display at the Smithsonian of Liars, Cheats, Abusers and Drug Addicts in Columbia. His grandma is hailed as an international hero. A gold statue was erected in her name right outside the Vatican.

Be your own hero. **Find a coping mechanism**.

Kevin the rapist unwillingly underwent a black market penectomy at the hands of an angry dad after knocking up a girl in high school. He has two pre-penis-removal daughters.

On a recent visit to Nairobi to secure a mail order bride, he ended up being mugged and then dragged behind a truck for attempting to steal a gold cross necklace for his new wife. They tossed him into the Sodomy Maximum Security Penitentiary in the Nairobi suburbs. Poor sap. **Don't be a victim**

Competition is flattery, in it's most sincere form, and it's vital to the scalability of your business.
The owner of Babysteals, at my last check in, was in the middle of **considering all of her possibilities, then adapting, or pivoting.**

I'm finally going to **know my competition,** even though she's no such thing anymore. **Sometimes winning is accepting that you didn't finish in first place and knowing you tried your hardest in the race for second,** and I'm happy for my first place running mate.

Never hire someone you wouldn't feel comfortable firing.
Becca, Jane and Hailey: These three. They tried their hands at beauty school. Their motto was 'Ugly is as ugly does'. When that venture failed only a week in, they decided to join a three-ring circus. All seemed swell, until they were caught shitting in the Emu nest they were hired to tend. **Hire slow—and fire fast.**

I'm not certain how anyone could fail at cleaning up animal feces, but somehow they'd managed. It's okay, girls, remember what I taught you, **persistence and patience.**

Usually when people put you down, it's a reflection of their own lack of self-confidence. It turns out Marie isn't even her mom's child—or her dad's. No one really knows where she came from. When she learned her mom was the mastermind behind 'PromiscuousUnlimited.god', a website catering to Church goers with an insatiable appetite for sex involving peanut butter, she packed up her nine kids and moved to the boonies. No one has heard from her since.

As for the woman she once knew as 'mom', a woman on a lifelong quest for her first orgasm, she married youth counselor, Jeff. Rumors say he has a fondness for intimacy with animals.

But most of all, I bet you're wondering what happened to the not so smart tech boys...

Those YUITS guys got themselves into a heap of shit. They apparently attempted to defraud another Internet company, Sewage Suckers United, an international company specializing in the cleanup of port-a-potty explosions. No one seems to have seen them since.

Legend has it, if you listen hard enough, when you shit in a portable toilet, you can hear their screams. These aren't brilliant people we're talking about here, folks.

Entrepreneurs should trust that the risks they're taking eventually pay off. Or fail. Don't allow yourself to be paralyzed by the fear of what ifs. I don't think YUITS' latest adventure could be considered a success. But who am I to judge? **Never assume**, I also, always say.

A little less satire:

Stanford and I promised each other we'd **always give the unabridged version**. He's not my better half, nor am I his. We are equal parts that have figured out how to complete one another.

We aren't necessarily always on the same page, but at least we are within the same chapter, and most certainly in the same book.

Just remember that **80% of everyone you know wants only 20% of your time, while the other 20% will try to poach the other 80%.** You get to decide which ones you give the most of yourself to.

Does your business love you back as much as your significant other does? Mine (business) didn't. It just took me six years to learn that **you can't give 100% to work/life balance, family and being an entrepreneur. Something will break**. I was broken.

There's more to life than loving and losing - there's living. There's also wine, and there's sex. And if you aren't having it regularly, you should probably get a checkup. Stanford and I smile with our therapist, laugh with our kids, and at each other.

Trust your gut. Our life isn't perfect - it's far from it, but we're happy. I get to worry about the simple things, now, like what temperature to cook the salmon at.

And the garden—what the hell should I do with 117 tomatoes?

And why do ten year olds still have temper tantrums?

Why does our five-year old flush my wallet down the toilet?

And how come our eight-year-old boy looks better in skinny jeans than I do?

There's a life I was missing out on—minute details in each day that I hadn't recognized.

My parents, the hornballs they are—inspire me. You aren't safe from my mom telling a dick joke or dad smacking her ass. You want to know something, though? Those two love each other, and it shows. Anyone in the same room with them can see it. They've been to hell and back, and their story is an inspiration. Maybe mom and I have butted heads because we're more alike than we ever wanted to admit? Who the fuck knows.

One thing is for certain—someday I'm going to be telling dirty jokes with my laughing adult kids present, and Stanford is going to be smacking my ass, still calling me 'babe'. It's going to disturb our kids. And I'm fucking okay with that.

If you're about to embark on starting a business of your own, remember three simple things:

* **The world is filled with 'Bill the jackasses'. Rise above them.**
* **Do not *just* be the CEO of your business, be the CEO of *your life*.**
* **There are no winners when a business closes. Not even one, ever.**

To begin to explain the depth of effort and support it took to put pen to paper, marker to dry erase board, and fingers to keyboard, would be a monumental task. Not one moment would've been possible without the support of Stanford, or that of my three boys and the many backup dancers that have graced my varying stages of life. Thank you.

My editor, Mark Staufer, who made me laugh, cry and scratch my head during the four years of writing this monstrosity. You've become a trusted confidante—thank you. And I still stand by the notion that in certain angles, you look just like my dad.

My parents, there are few words available in the English language that could begin describe the depth of love and gratitude I have for each of you. #lifegoals

My blind taste-testers, beta readers and critique-givers, thank you for not going easy on me.

Lastly, and most certainly not least—every single customer, client, employee or consultant that loved, championed, loathed or bashed Mamabargains—whether you realize it or not, each of you has made a deep, life-long and positive impact on my entire being. Thank you, deeply and sincerely.

<<<<>>>>

Made in the USA
San Bernardino, CA
02 February 2019